YOUR KNOWLEDGE HAS VALUE

Eva-Maria Krapfenbauer

The same old story? The portrayal of gender and ethnicity/race in Disney movies and the possible (re-) production of stereotypes over the course of the past 75 years

GRIN Publishing

Bibliographic information published by the German National Library:

The German National Library lists this publication in the National Bibliography;
detailed bibliographic data are available on the Internet at http://dnb.dnb.de .

Imprint:

Copyright © 2013 GRIN Verlag GmbH
Print and binding: Books on Demand GmbH, Norderstedt Germany
ISBN: 978-3-656-85908-6

This book at GRIN:

http://www.grin.com/en/e-book/284783/the-same-old-story-the-portrayal-of-gender-
and-ethnicity-race-in-disney

GRIN - Your knowledge has value

Since its foundation in 1998, GRIN has specialized in publishing academic texts by students, college teachers and other academics as e-book and printed book. The website www.grin.com is an ideal platform for presenting term papers, final papers, scientific essays, dissertations and specialist books.

Visit us on the internet:

http://www.grin.com/

http://www.facebook.com/grincom

http://www.twitter.com/grin_com

gender and
diversity in
organizations

WIRTSCHAFTS
UNIVERSITÄT
WIEN VIENNA
UNIVERSITY OF
ECONOMICS
AND BUSINESS

Bachelor's Thesis

The same old story?

Taking a closer look at the portrayal of gender and ethnicity/race in Disney movies and the possible (re-) production of stereotypes over the course of the past 75 years.

Verfasserin

Eva-Maria Krapfenbauer

angestrebter akademischer Grad

Bachelor of Science (BSc)

Studienrichtung lt. Studienblatt: Wirtschafts- und Sozialwissenschaften
Studienzweig: Internationale Betriebswirtschaftslehre

Institut: Abteilung für Gender- und Diversitätsmanagement

Kurzzusammenfassung

Die folgende Bachelorarbeit behandelt die (Re-)Produktion von genderbezogenen und ethnischen Stereotypen in den Animationsfilmen des Disney Prinzessinnen Franchises. Der Einleitung zum Thema folgt eine Darlegung der Theorie, welche die Konzepte Diversität, Gender und Ethnizität vorstellt, sowie eine kurze Einführung in Stereotypen beinhaltet. Im Literaturteil wird der Konzern Disney präsentiert sowie die Themen Fernsehen und Kinderfernsehen abgehandelt. Des Weiteren werden dort die bisherigen Forschungsergebnisse zu dem Themenbereich „Disney, Gender und Ethnizität" vorgestellt. Danach folgt eine Vorstellung der kritischen Diskursanalyse und der Methodologie. Das Anschlusskapitel beinhaltet den empirischen Teil mit der Analyse und Diskussion der Filme. In der abschließenden Konklusion werden die Ergebnisse sowohl zusammengeführt als auch mit den anderen Teilen der Arbeit in Bezug gesetzt.

Schlagworte: Disney, Prinzessinnen Franchise, Gender, Rasse, Ethnizität, Stereotypen, Kinderfernsehen

Abstract

The following Bachelor's thesis deals with the (re-)production of gender-related and ethnic stereotypes in animated movies part of the Disney Princess franchise. The introduction to the topic is followed by an overview of the theory, which includes the concepts of diversity, gender, and ethnicity as well as an introduction into stereotypes. The literature review will on the one hand present the Disney corporation and on the other hand give insight into the topics of television in general and children's television in particular. It also outlines the hitherto findings pertaining to the scientific field of "Disney, gender and ethnicity". The next chapters contain an introduction to the Critical Discourse Analysis and the methodology, which is followed by the empirical part consisting of the analysis and discussion of the movies. The thesis is completed by the conclusion, which brings together the findings as well as putting them in relation to the rest of the thesis.

Key words: Disney, Princess Franchise, Gender, Race, Ethnicity, Stereotypes, Children's TV

Danksagung

Das Verfassen dieser Bachelorarbeit war nicht nur aus akademischer Sicht meine bisher größte Herausforderung, sondern hat mich auch persönlich in vielerlei Hinsicht sehr gefordert - manchmal fast schon überfordert. Die Arbeit wurde zu einem Projekt, welches sehr viel Spaß und Freude in mein Leben brachte, aber auch viele Zweifel und Rückschläge. Dass sie schlussendlich fertiggestellt wurde, ist eine große Genugtuung und Bestätigung, allerdings war es nicht mein Verdienst alleine. Daher möchte ich diese Stelle nutzen, um *Danke* zu sagen.

Danke an meine Eltern und meinen Bruder, die mich auf meinem Weg immer bestärkt und unterstützt und die mir all das ermöglicht haben. Sie gaben mir die Ruhe und die Zeit diese Arbeit zu schreiben und hatten stets Vertrauen in meine Fähigkeiten, selbst wenn ich es nicht hatte.

Danke an Julia und Viola, die mich immer unterstützt haben wenn ich nicht mehr konnte, und mir einen Tritt in den Hintern gegeben haben, wenn ich nicht mehr wollte. Und für ihr Verständnis, dass ich dieser Bachelorarbeit sehr viel von unserer gemeinsamen Zeit geopfert habe.

Danke möchte ich auch meiner Betreuerin Regine Bendl sagen, welche mir durch ihre Ruhe und Gelassenheit den nötigen Raum und die Zeit für das Schreiben der Arbeit gab, deren Rückmeldungen stets direkt und zielgerichtet waren und welche mich mit Lob und Verständnis dort auffing, wo ich zwischendurch etwas verloren war.

Und schließlich *Danke* an alle meine Freunde, Freundinnen und Bekannte, welche mir in vielen Gesprächen immer wieder neuen Input und neue Motivation gegeben haben.

Table of contents

Table of figures

Table of charts

Table of abbreviations

CDA   ...   Critical Discourse Analysis

WHR   ...   waist-to-hip ratio

WSR   ...   waist-to-shoulder ratio

UB/LB...   upper body – lower body ratio

1. Introduction

The goal of this Bachelor's thesis is to analyze, whether the (re-)presentation of women and men as well as different ethnic groups in Disney movies has changed over the course of time.

Seeing how Disney has grown into the biggest and most prominent children's entertainment caterer, the contents and messages broadcasted to them warrant a closer look.

During my research for this Bachelor's thesis, I have been introduced to the basic concepts of 'discourse'. I have learned a lot about its mode of operation, about how it is created, by what it may be affected and how it affects individuals and society as a whole. The framework of 'discourse' combined with a critical view of the Disney Company itself (and not just the movies) contribute greatly not only to the findings in this thesis, but also to understanding *why* it is important to take a closer look into this topic and not just accept Disney films as products of fantasy and imagination.

Henry A. Giroux (1995, http://www.henryagiroux.com/online_articles/ animating_youth.htm), who is one of the founding theorists of critical pedagogy in the United States, wrote: "*Children's culture as an object of critical analysis opens up a space in which children become an important dimension of social theory. While youth culture, especially adolescence, has been a strong component of cultural studies, children's culture has been largely ignored, especially the world of animated films.*" It seems, that "*popular audiences are more willing to suspend critical judgement about such children's films.*" However, the influence of animated films in general and Disney movies in particular should not be underestimated.

Feng and Scharrer (2004) conducted a study among college students in order to test whether they would change their attitudes towards the 1991 Disney film *The Little Mermaid* after a critical review. In a university course the students were introduced to the tale by Andersen, which the movie was based on, and deconstructed the gender roles and stereotypes presented in the movie. Their results were enlightening and frightening at the same time. "*[T]hey did not want to change their attitudes about Disney's* The

Little Mermaid, *which has given them intense pleasure and fond memories since they were children, and they articulated a few strategies which enabled them to uphold their previously existing opinions. They ignored or dismissed the criticism as "overdone" [...]. They said that they liked the film too much to allow criticism to affect them [...]. [O]ne-fifth of the respondents said that though they acknowledged problems with Disney's* The Little Mermaid, *they could also suspend their criticism while watching the film and, therefore, still enjoy it.*" (Feng & Scharrer, 2004, p. 51)

The underlying assumption I present in this thesis, is that Disney always has and still is portraying very conservative role models of gender and certain ethnic groups. Therefore, it introduces and re-affirms outdated stereotypes to our children, which may influence them negatively in their development and helps in perpetuating social inequalities. Given that children are Disney's target group combined with the fact that they are more easily influenced by what they see on television, the messages presented to them have to be carefully studied and analyzed.

Considering all the above, I formulated the following research question: "How is/was gender and ethnicity portrayed in (chosen) Disney feature-length films and how do these portrayals reproduce stereotypes?"

While there has been plenty of research in this field already (Artz, 2007; Ayres, 2003; LaCroix 2004, Manley 2003), most studies and essays only deal with singular movies or particular aspects of diversity. Scientific papers that compare several movies and take a closer look at the possible development in Disney storytelling are fewer (Yzaguirre 2006, Matyas 2010). However, Disney has produced films for a very long time, which allows us to take a closer look at whether Disney has progressed when it comes to the contents and messages distributed by its films or not.

At first glance, the presented literature review may seem disjointed and incoherent. However, this new approach to analyzing the different pieces of gender and ethnic representation in Disney movies is the strength of this thesis. Put together, each one of the topics introduces information, which will be essential to understanding why it is important to consider Disney movies carefully.

As I will illustrate in the theoretical part, gender and ethnicity/race are something given (as in compared to e.g. life-style choices) and are not something we can easily (if at all) change about ourselves. Yet, it is because of these (perceived) differences that people are being treated and valued differently. Therefore, it is indispensable to change the social perception of diversity and turn it into something we celebrate rather than discriminate. In order to achieve this, we have to alter the public discourse on diversity.

The thesis started with the problem statement and the research question to establish the significance of this topic. The theoretical part and the literature review serve to give an overview of the very diverse aspects pertaining to this topic. It will introduce the reader to different concepts, which can be seen as different pieces belonging to the same puzzle. The reader will be familiarised with the concepts of diversity, gender and ethnicity/race. In addition, the basics of stereotyping in general and gender and racial/ethnic stereotyping in particular will be outlined. The literature review starts with an insight into the Disney Company as well as the Disney Princess franchise. Furthermore, the relevant literature on television's effect on children and the representation of gender and ethnicity/race in children's television will be presented. The last part of the literature review will give an overview of the hitherto findings connected to the topics of Disney movies, gender, and ethnicity/race. The next chapter will introduce the reader to the basic framework of Critical Discourse Analysis and its underlying concepts, since I have chosen the Critical Discourse Analysis as my method to conduct my study. After explaining my methodology, I present and discuss the findings of my analysis. The conclusion will bring the pieces together and points to possible future areas of research.

2. Theory

This chapter will explain the concept of diversity and how the different dimensions of diversity influence us in our being and in our (everyday) life. Furthermore, we will take a closer look at the two diversity-dimensions 'gender' and 'ethnicity/race', because the analysis in this thesis focuses on these particular dimensions. Also, there will be a short introduction into stereotyping and an overview of gender stereotypes and ethnic/racial stereotypes.

2.1. Diversity

Although the expression "diversity" is vague and can mean and refer to various things[1], nowadays it is most commonly used to point out the differences in people. One of the definitions offered by the online dictionary Merriam-Webster[2] is: *"the condition of having or being composed of differing elements: variety; especially: the inclusion of different types of people (as people of different races or cultures) in a group or organization, <programs intended to promote diversity in schools>"*. Schlote and Götz (2010) further explain that in this context diversity can also refer to the economic, cultural and social differences between people. The exact definition of the term "diversity" and what it encompasses is always dependent on the context. (Schlote & Götz, 2010, p. 8)

In this thesis, I conceptualize diversity in the following way: *"Diversity [is] representing a multitude of individual differences and similarities that exist among people. Diversity can encompass many different human characteristics such as race, age, creed, national origin, religion, ethnicity or sexual orientation."* (Wellner 2000, as cited in Washington 2008, p. 3)

One of the most widely used concepts or tools to define and illustrate diversity is Gardenswartz's and Rowe's (see Gardenswartz & Rowe, 2009, p. 36) "Four Layers of Diversity Model". In this model (see figure 1), different layers of diversity are being defined.

---

[1] See a list at http://en.wikipedia.org/wiki/Diversity
[2] http://www.merriam-webster.com/dictionary/diversity

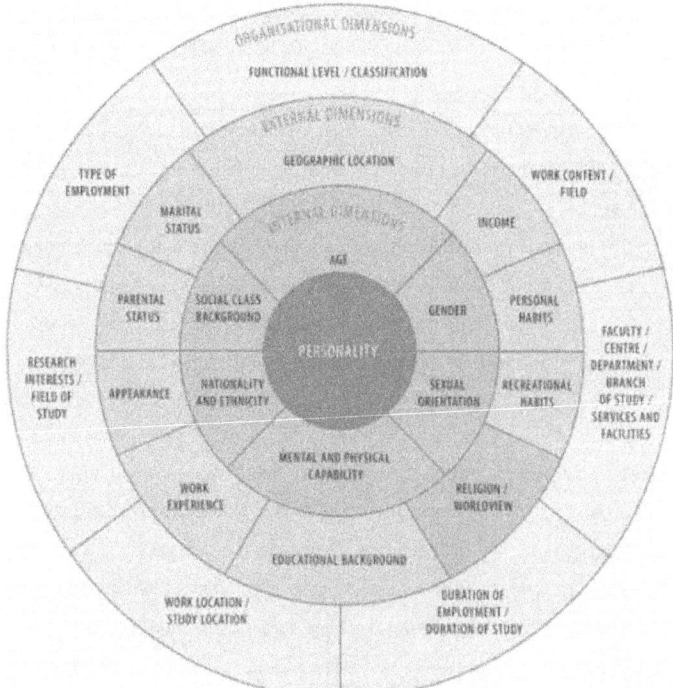

Figure 1: see Gardenswartz, L. &. Rowe, A.: Diverse Teams at Work; Society for Human Resource Management 2002; Source: University of Vienna http://www.univie.ac.at/diversity/146.html

The centre – Personality – relates to individual style and characteristics of a person.

The second layer – Internal Dimension – comprises gender, age, sexual orientation, race, ethnicity and physical ability. Gardenswartz and Rowe (2009) argue that we have little control over these aspects of our personality, meaning they are not choices we make, but yet define how our environment treats us and what people expect of us, as well as what we expect of ourselves.

The next layer – External Dimensions – encompasses aspects such as religion, education, marital status, work experience, and recreational habits. These aspects are choices we make and therefore we have more influence over them. Religion/Worldview is offered a 'special' position, as it is argued that sometimes we cannot freely choose or change our faith.

The last layer – Organizational Dimensions – contains aspects of similarity and difference that are part of the working environment in an organization.

Although this model is primarily used within a management and business context, it is of good use in this thesis, because it gives a concise overview on diversity in all its facets. All the aspects illustrated represent areas, in which people may find similarities as well as differences. We will see that these differences are crucial to stereotyping.

2.1.1. Gender

Gender usually references to the sex of a person, therefore distinguishing between men and women according to their anatomical difference. Subsequently, there are two genders: male and female, man and woman. Gender in the diversity discourse, however, refers to what is thought to be appropriately male and female, therefore adverting *"cultural assumptions and practices that govern the social construction of men, women and their social relations."* In this sense, sex is the biological formation of the body, while in contrast gender points to the cultural and social expectations, regulations and limitations a person will experience based on their sex. Put differently, sex is a biological expression while gender has morphed into a social expression, *"[g]iven that gender is held to be a matter of culture rather than 'nature', [...]"*. (see Bloomsbury Guide to Human Thought; retrieved from http://www.credoreference.com/entry/bght/genders, 2012)

The above description of gender points to the sex-gender distinction, which has been predominant in feminist literature for the past decades. However, recently this sex-gender distinction itself has become the subject of criticism. Judith Butler (1990) has suggested that the category of 'sex' is part of a normative and regulatory discourse which produces the bodies it governs. Although 'sex' is a biological category, it is always discussed within cultural discourse and therefore, *"sexed bodies are always already represented as the production of regulatory discourses"* (Butler, 1990, as cited in Bloomsbury Guide to Human Thought; retrieved from http://www.credoreference.com/entry/bght/genders, 2012).

Connell (2000) further illustrates this argument by explaining that there is a pattern in our social arrangements and the everyday activities and practices they govern. These extensive and – above all - enduring patterns among our social relations are called 'structures" in social theory. Hence, gender cannot be understood as an expression of biology, but neither in a fixed dichotomy in human life or character. Therefore she offers the following definition: *"Gender is the structure of social relations that centres on the reproductive arena, and the set of practices (governed by this structure) that bring reproductive distinctions between bodies into social processes. To put it informally, gender concerns the way human society deals with human bodies, and the many consequences of that 'dealing' in our personal lives and our collective fate"* (Connell, 2000, p. 10).

2.1.2. Race & Ethnicity

When it comes to defining the terms 'race' and 'ethnicity' it is important to know that they have no fixed referents. (Author's note: Referent is a linguistic expression, which describes a tangible object, to which a linguistic expression refers to.[3]) Rather, the conventions of naming and defining these terms are constantly changing. The fact that the terms 'race' and 'ethnicity' have different meanings at differnt moments in time also highlights the fact that they refer to socially constructed concepts. Hence, 'race' and 'ethnicity' belong to the domain of shifting social and cultural meanings in which boundaries are constantly negotiated. (see Spencer, 2006, p. 32)

The process of defining the terms is so important and challenging, because the categorizing and subsequent labelling of a group of individuals is a highly sensitive area due to its political and social implications. Setting those boundaries form the basis of inclusion and exclusion. It may on the one hand allow for individual choice and self-determination or on the other enforce dominant culture, colonial power or government. This situation of ever-evolving expressions and the lack of a definite denotation also lead to many issues in everyday life about what the (politically) correct terms to describe ethnic groups are. (see Spencer, 2006, p. 32)

---

[3] http://dict.leo.org/forum/viewUnsolvedquery.php?idThread=544420&idForum=2&lp=ende&lang=de

However, *"[t]he modernist connotation of 'race' and 'ethnicity' sees 'race' either subsumed in 'ethnicity', or referret to euphemistically through 'ethnicity'"* (Popeau 1998, p. 177, as cited in Spencer 2006, p. 32) and *"the term 'ethnicity' is typically used as a 'polite' and less controversial term for 'race'"* (Popeau, 1998, p. 166, as cited in Spencer, 2006, p. 32).

Spencer (2006) suggests that in the modern era, ethnicity is generally used as term for collective cultural identity. He argues that while a group would use the term race to categorize 'them' from the outside, ethnicity is applied to point to shared values and beliefs. Hence it defines the group, the 'us'. He cites Van den Berghe, who *"drew the influential distinction between ethnicity as 'socially defined but on the basis of cultural criteria' whereas race is 'socially defined but on the basis of physical criteria'"* (Van den Berghe, 1967, p. 9, as cited in Spencer, 2006, p. 45). Based on this distinction we can draw the conclusion that 'ethnicity' is a more inclusive and less objectifying conept than 'race' and therefore has become the preferred term. (see Spencer, 2006, p. 45)

2.1.3. Ethnic Minorities

To highlight why the concept of 'race' and 'ethnicity' and its representation in mass media is so important, I want to refer to the concept of 'ethnic minorities'. 'Minorities' in general *"are disadvantaged ethnic, national, religious, linguistic or cultural groups who are smaller in number than the rest of the population and who may wish to maintain and develop their identity"* (Minority Rights Group International, 2009, as cited in Schlote, 2010, p. 14; see also http://www.minorityrights.org/566/who-are-minorities/who-are-minorities.html).

James D. Fearon conducted a study on ethnic minorities. To be considered in his results, the groups had to have at least the size of 1% of a country's population. He further differentiated between dimensions of diversity: ethnic diversity[4] and linguistic diversity[5]. Applying these restrictions, Fearon distinguished 822 ethnic groups in 160 countries.

---

[4] *"To differentiate between groups, he (note: Fearon) used diverse ethnic and cultural markers: people who share the same descent, have a common language, religion and customs. Ideally, members and non-members should recognize this grouping as an ethnic group."* (Schlote, 2010, p. 14)
[5] *"Fearon compared different languages and cultural proximity of the languages for every country."* (Schlote, 2010, p. 14)

The resulting illustration (see figure 2) *"shows the ethnic-cultural and linguistic diversi-ty in some selected countries. A higher score indicates a more diverse population con-sisting of different ethnic groups"*[6] (Schlote, 2010, p. 14).

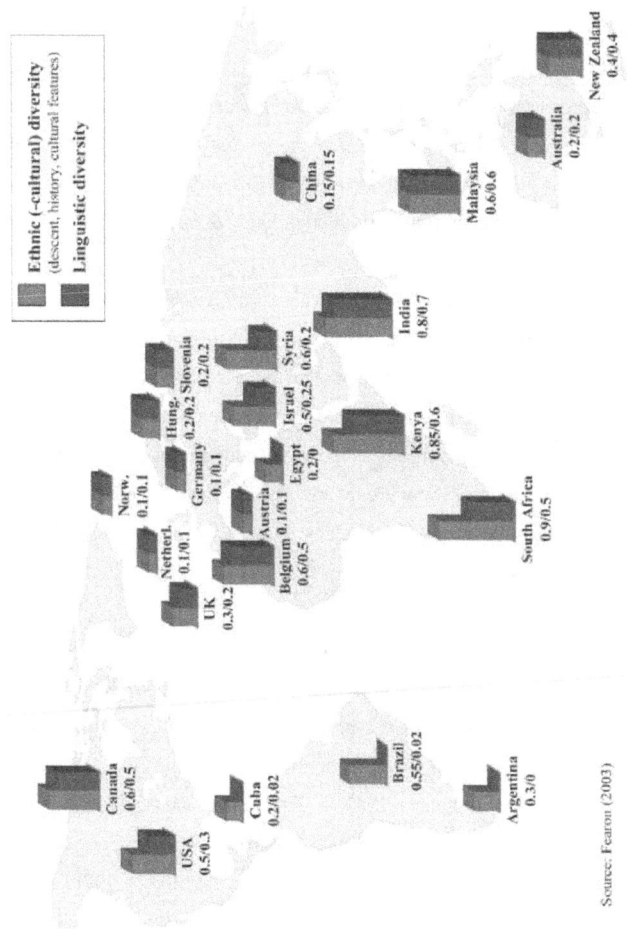

Figure 2: Illustration of ethnic-cultural and linguistic diversity in selected countries. Source: Televizion magazine (23/2010/E), Schlote (2010, p. 14) based on Fearon (2003)

---

[6] *"Fearon states explicitly that his work, which is based on data from secondary sources from the 1990s, should be viewed as work in progress."* (Schlote, 2010, p. 14)

The above chart serves to illustrate that we do live in a multicultural and diverse society in which the concepts of inclusion and visible (re-)presentation in mass media become increasingly important.

2.2. Stereotypes

"[...] [L]ike other social stereotypes, reflect perceivers' observations of what people do in daily life. If perceivers often observe a particular group of people engaging in a particular activity, they are likely to believe that the abilities and personality attributes required to carry out that activity are typical of that group of people." (Feldman 1972, Smedley & Bayton 1978, Triandis 1977, as cited in Eagly & Steffen, 1984, p. 735)

For example, people believe that characteristics necessary for childrearing and childcare are nurturance and warmth. Thus, if women are constantly seen caring for children, then perceivers will probably be prone to believe that these characteristics are typical for women. However, as we have established before, most people's activities are linked to their assigned social roles which means stereotypes about a group of people is more a reflection of the distribution of these groups into social roles than a description of the people themselves. (see Feldman 1972, Smedley & Bayton 1978, Triandis 1977, as cited in Eagly & Steffen, 1984, p. 735)

A process of categorizing precedes the process of stereotyping. *"Perception involves an act of categorization. [...] [A]ll perceptual experience is necessarily the end product of a categorization process."* (Bruner, 1957, p. 124) We apply this process of categorization not only to objects but also to people. It helps us simplify our complex social environment. (see Allport 1954, Lippmann 1922, Tajfel 1969, as cited in Dotsch 2011, p. 1) Categories serve to gain and access information about our environment while at the same time help saving energy and conserving resources. (see Rosch 1978) Rosch and Lloyd call this "cognitive economy" (Rosch, 1978, p. 3).

McGarty et al. (2002) offer three guiding principles for stereotyping. Firstly, they believe stereotypes are aids to explanation. This means, stereotypes help us make sense of a situation. Secondly, they describe stereotypes as energy-saving devices. This goes in accordance with Rosch and Lloyd (1978), as it implies that stereotypes reduce the effort needed to process our environment. Thirdly, stereotypes act as shared group beliefs, which means they should be formed in accordance with the accepted views or norms of social groups that the perceiver belongs to. (see McGarty et al., 2002, p. 3)

These principles offered by McGarty et al. (2002) imply a rather positive function of stereotypes, however Brannon (2000, p. 160) points out that stereotypes *"can be very powerful forces in judgments of self and others"* and Prentice and Carranza (2002, p. 269) further warn of stereotypes being *"highly prescriptive"*.

2.2.1. Gender Stereotypes

The concept of gender roles and gender stereotypes tend to be related, in that gender roles lay the basis for gender stereotypes. (see Brannon, 2000, p. 160)

Gender roles consist of activities that men and women engage in with different frequencies, thus these gender-related behaviours become part of a pattern accepted as masculine or feminine. This happens not because of any innate or nature-given reason for differences between men and women, but because of the associations with women and men. Therefore, gender roles can be defined as and are defined by behaviours typically shown by women and men. (see Brannon, 2000, p. 160)

Gender stereotypes, on the other hand, are beliefs about attitudes of masculinity and femininity. They build on ideas about the psychological traits and characteristics of, as well as the activities and manners appropriate to, women or men. They act as an agent in conceptualizing and defining the terms "woman" and "man" and consequently establish social categories for gender. Hence, gender stereotypes are very influential forces in our judgment of ourselves, others and our environment. (see Brannon 2000, p. 160)

Furthermore, gender stereotypes are not only descriptive, but in addition highly prescriptive as well. The qualities and abilities attributed to women and men respectively are likely to be the ones also required of women and men. Prentice and Carranza (2002) carried out a study to identify the most common traits associated with women and men. Although their results did not differ highly from previous studies, they highlighted and emphasised that old-fashioned images of what a woman or a man should be continue to persist in our society: *"The intensified prescriptions and proscriptions for women re-*

flected traditional emphases on interpersonal sensitivity, niceness, modesty, and socia-bility, whereas the intensified prescriptions and proscriptions for men reflected tradi-tional emphases on strength, drive, assertiveness, and self-reliance. Moreover, the vast majority of these traits showed corresponding differences in the extent to which they were perceived as typical of women and men." (Prentice & Carranza, 2002, p. 272)

In addition, *"[...] the results indicate that people believe women and men to differ in most of the ways they are supposed to differ"* (Prentice & Carranza, 2002, p. 272). This analysis is helpful in understanding that gender stereotypes persist, because people be-lieve they are *supposed to* exist. Connell (2000, p. 54) illustrates that *"[g]ender rela-tions are always being constituted in everyday life. If we don't bring it into being, gen-der does not exist."*

2.2.2. Racial Stereotypes

Much of what has been said about gender stereotypes can also be applied to racial stere-otypes, the most important being that racial stereotypes are based on what *we believe* are differences between ethnic groups rather than actually existing differences (or simi-larities). Taijfel's (1981, p. 116) definition of racial stereotypes supports this argument: *"A stereotype about an ethnic group is generally defined in terms of a consensus of opinion concerning the traits attributed to that group. If subjects are presented with a list of attributes and asked to indicate those which they believe apply to a specific group, those chosen most frequently can be assumed to belong to the culturally held stereotype".*

As we can gather from this, racial stereotypes are based in the shared belief of one eth-nic group about another. Since these stereotypes are heavily dependent on the cultural background of an individual, they are not only different for every group to which they are applied to, but they will as well be different according to the groups that apply them. Therefore I will not go into further detail here, but will point to specific racial stereo-types (and prejudices) in the analysis of the movies itself.

The above presented concepts serve as a framework for the following literature review. It serves to show that 'diversity' plays an important part in our life and has a lot of in-fluence on our life and our actions. A great deal of this influence stems from the (often negative) stereotypes connected to those diversity dimensions. Therefore, a first important step is to be aware of those stereotypes, in order to abolish them.

3. Literature Review

The literature review will give a brief overview of research already conducted within this particular field of interest. The first part of the chapter will give a short introduction into television in general, before dealing with children's television in particular. The second part of the chapter gives a few facts and numbers on the Disney Corporation and the Disney Princess franchise. The third part connects the first two parts and will give an outline on academic research on gender and ethnicity/race in Disney movies.

3.1. Television

Nowadays, television is to be considered a learning environment. Movies and TV shows have an inherent story-telling function, which has become extremely important. In order to fulfil the task of storytelling, television has developed into a *"wholesale distributer of images and the mainstream of our popular culture"*. It is through the stories seen and heard on television that people learn about the world and the people in it. (see Signorielli, 1993, p. 229)

The world of television shows and tells us about life, including people, places, striving, power, and fate. It presents the good and bad, the happy and sad, and lets us know who is successful and who a failure. (see Signorielli 1993, p. 229)

3.2. Children & Television

Although children of every generation have always been faced with change and progress happening around them, nowadays they are presented with a special challenge. Today, children are growing up in a society driven by various forms of media. This realization is of importance *"because television and its electronic relations seem to play a role, albeit one sometimes difficult to identify, in the socialisation process"* of our children. (see Berry & Asamen, 1993, p. 5)

Murray (1993, p. 9) points to the fact that television reaches children at a much earlier age than other media before or since. Due to its central role in our multimedia environment, it reaches not only adults but also children with greater intensity. As children are more impressionable, this increases the potential of television to influence not only the intellectual, but also the emotional development of children immensely. Signorielli (1993) argues that television may be the most suitable media of all for (children's) socialization. Nowadays, scholars (Hawkins & Pingree 1986, Houston & Wright 1989, as cited in Fitch et al., 1993, p. 38) have established the view that television is a medium, which conveys meaning by means of content and form and *"that children are active processors of the medium"*. This means that children use content as well as form *"to interpret television's messages"*.

3.3. Gender & Ethnicity/Race in Children's TV

"In order to attain Barbie's figure (classic edition) a woman would have to be between 6' 2" and 7'4" tall or have one rib removed. From a medical point of view she would very likely be suffering from a slipped disc, respiratory problems, and osteoporosis; moreover, she would be infertile: Certainly a very unhealthy person." (Herche & Götz, 2008, p. 18)

Seeing the bulk of skinny female characters on children's TV – especially those broadcasted on a global scale - Herche and Götz (2008) analysed the bodies of 102 animated girl and female young adult characters in order to examine their body measurements. Their results are rather sobering. They used stills of full frontal views and took measurements of the hips, waist, shoulders, and height in order to calculate a waist-to-hip ratio (WHR), a waist-to-shoulder ratio (WSR) and an upper body – lower body ratio (UB/LB).

The waist-to-shoulder ratio for a slim, healthy, young woman would range between 0.69 and 0.80. However, their study showed that this value only applies to 16% of the cartoon characters, while all the other characters fall below that value. The waist-to-hip ratio for a slim, healthy, young woman would be between 0.69 and 0.80 as well. However, as can be seen in the figure below, over half of the cartoon characters (58%) have a value below, which means it is not naturally achievable.

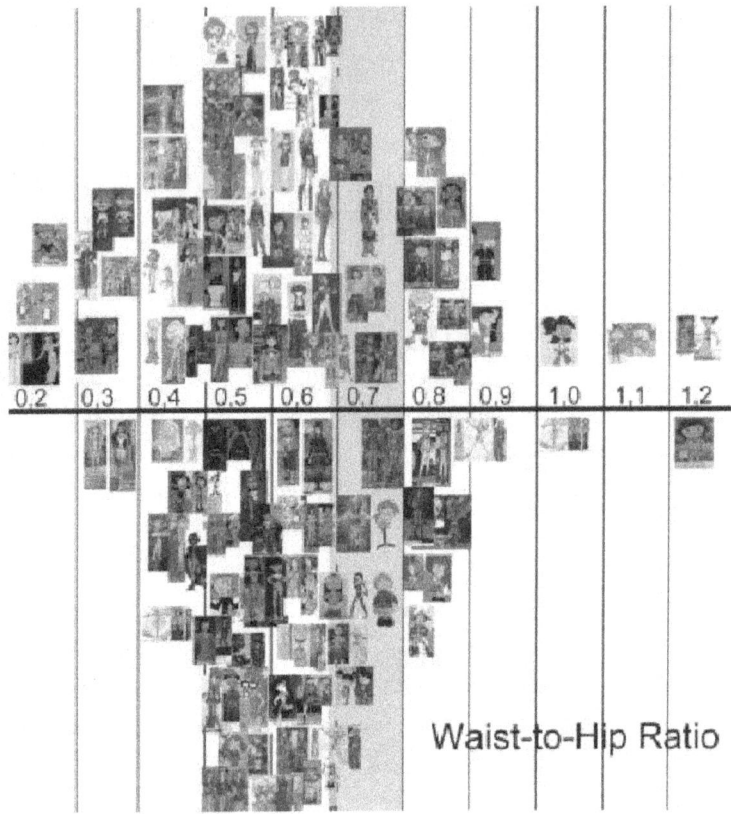

Figure 3: Distribution of 102 female TV cartoon characters according to their waist-to-hip ratios; the blue column indicates a normal and healthy WHR. Source: Herche & Götz, 2008, p. 18 in Televizion magazine (21/2008/E)

Combining these two ratios, most presented bodies have an unnaturally small waist. These so-called "wasp waists" are not only unhealthy, they would even remain unattainable through cosmetic surgery. In addition, Herche and Götz (2008, p. 18) emphasise another problem: *"The problem involved here is not only the impossibility of the goal, but also the sexualisation that goes along with it. [...] The presented body formulas of the animated girl characters, then, do not represent child or young girl characters, but instead little girls' bodies that have been sexualised, or, put more simply: "Girls as sex bombs". In the domain of children's TV, though, this hardly seems appropriate or sensible."*

The third ratio they calculated – the upper body-to-lower body ratio – presented problematic results again. Young women would have an upper body-to-lower body ratio between 0.32 and 0.42. Their results showed, that 57% have legs, which are longer than could ever be reached naturally, and *"[n]early every third character has legs longer than even Barbie's"* (Herche & Götz, 2008, p. 19).

In the same study, Herche and Götz (2008) also analysed the bodies of 71 boy and men characters, which are broadcasted globally. They examined their shoulder-to-waist ratio in order to judge the V-shape of their torsos. The V-shape of the male torso is described as the equivalent to the female "wasp waist". Their results show, that there is *"a range of male characters with V-shaped torsos, like one could only achieve by working out professionally for years"* (Herche & Götz, 2008, p. 19). However, their results also indicate that the range of differently shaped bodies (ballshaped bodies, "beanpoles", normal bodies) is considerably wider than with female characters. In addition, the number of male characters who are not sexualised is higher as well (see figure below).

In their conclusion, Herche and Götz (2008) argue that these results demonstrate an overbearing presence of unhealthy role models for children – especially young girls – on global TV. The bodies of the animated characters are not only overly sexualised, but in many cases could only be attained by undergoing cosmetic surgery or damaging one's health. This can be very damaging to young girls, because *"[v]arious studies have clearly demonstrated that body schemata especially are adopted as inner images. The reduction of the beauty ideal to an overly slim body and the increasing discontent with one's own appearance are inevitable consequences, because, compared with those of the female TV characters, one's own body can only be regarded as deficient"* (Herche & Götz, 2008, p. 19).

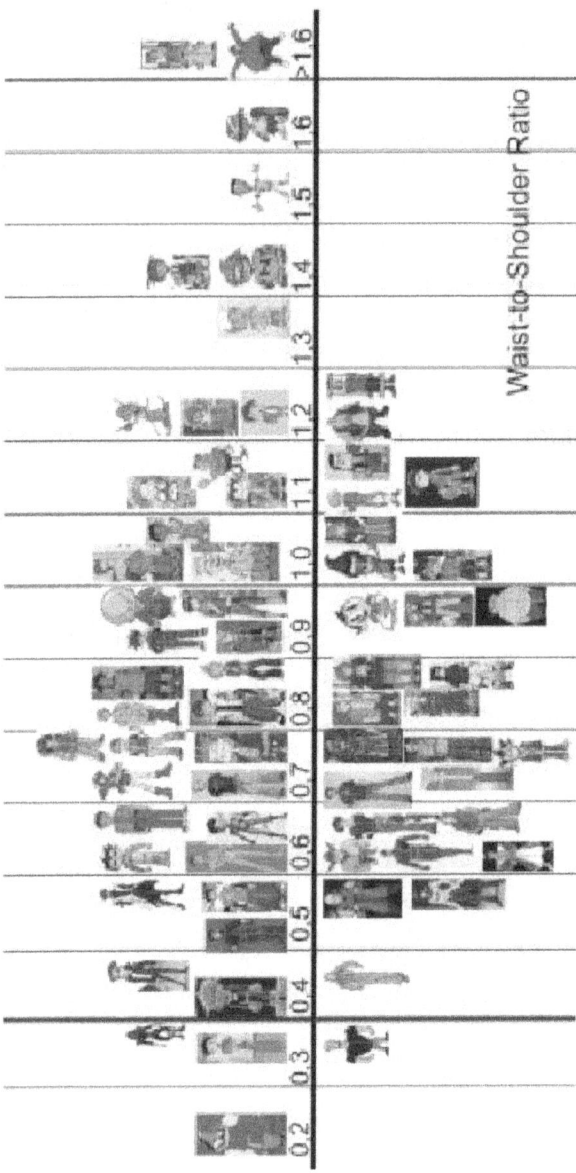

Figure 4: Distribution of 71 male TV cartoon characters according to their waist-to-shoulder ratios; a ratio below the blue line is not naturally achievable. Source: Herche & Götz, 2008, p. 19 in Televizion magazine (21/2008/E)

In a media analysis conducted across 24 nations, Götz et al. (2008) examined the main characters of fictional TV programmes. Their results showed *"a clear underrepresentation and stereotyped depiction of female characters worldwide"* (Götz et al., 2008, p. 4).

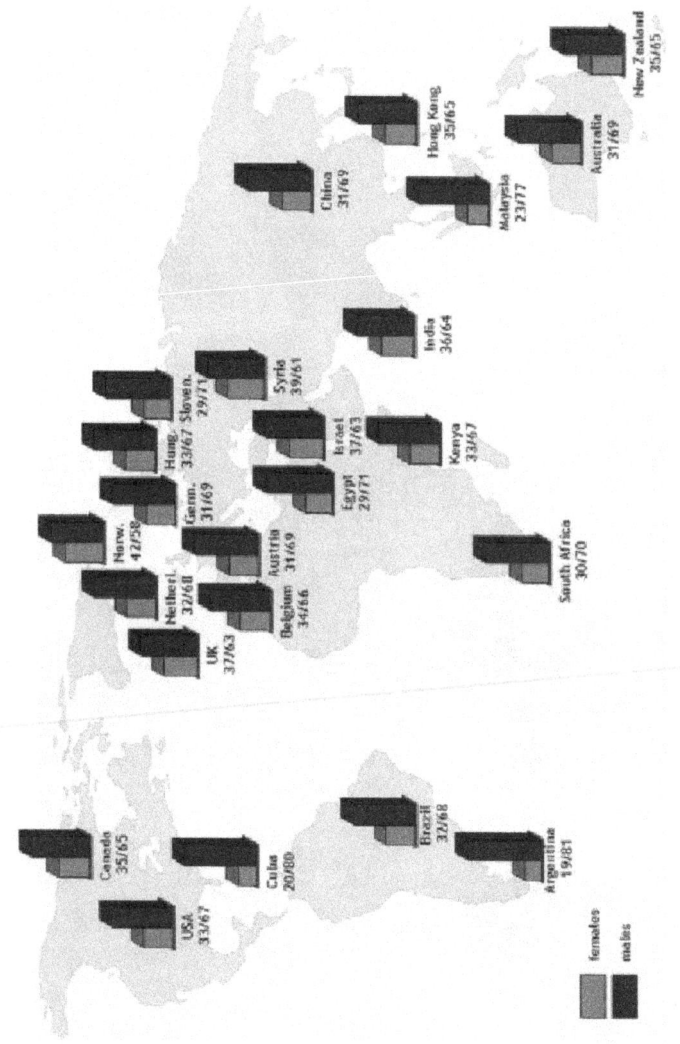

Figure 5: Percentage distribution of male and female main characters in fictional shows on children's TV in selected countries, Source: Götz et al., 2008, p. 6 in Televizion magazine (21/2008/E)

In detail, their conclusion shows that there are *"more than twice as many male charac-*
ters than female characters on children's TV" (see figure above). In addition, *"72 % of*
all main characters are Caucasian and in most of the countries the reality of ethnic di-
versity is not represented in an appropriate way" (see figure below). Furthermore are
"[o]verweight girls or elderly women [...] virtually absent" and while females are often
depicted in groups, males are presented as loners and antagonists (Götz et al., 2008, p.
8).

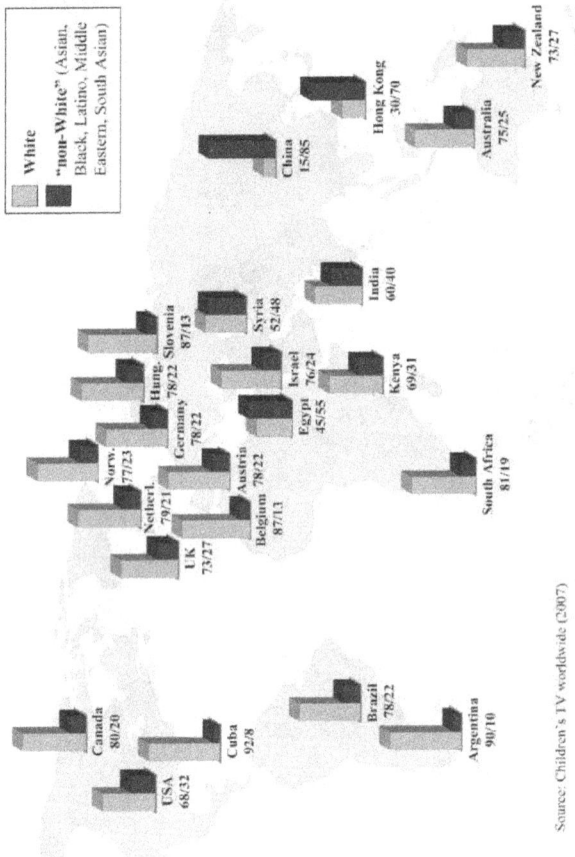

Figure 6: Percentage distribution of main characters with white skin colour and non-
white skin colour in selected countries, Source: Schlote & Otremba, 2010, p. 9 in Televizion magazine (23/2010/2)

The above information combined with the charts clearly show that the content broadcasted on children's TV does not mirror social realities. Bearing in mind that TV is nowadays a mass-media, frequently used by children and which in general has great influence on their world-views and self-perception, this information helps to understand why we have to take a closer look at Disney movies in particular, since Disney has a very powerful position in the children's entertainment sector.

3.4. The Walt Disney Corporation

This chapter will give key information about Disney as a company and shows the most important dates, numbers, and figures. While at first thought this may seem out of context in this thesis, it is imperative to first present Disney for what it is – a business, which's primary goal is to maximise profits.

Wasko (2001, p. 245) wrote in her paper on the 5 biggest myths surrounding Disney: *"It is still difficult for many fans, as well as academics, to think of the Disney company as a profit-motivated corporation. The company is thought to be somehow different or special, not tainted with the attributes of other corporations and their money-grubbing policies. Challenging this myth involves understanding Disney as a capitalist enterprise, [...]."*

The information presented in this chapter was taken from a company profile created by MarketLine. MarketLine *"offers a comprehensive and unique collection of company, industry, financial, product and country information, research and data extending across every major marketplace and industry"*. (MarketLine, www.marketline.com)

3.4.1. Business History

The Walt Disney Company's History starts in the year 1923, when the two brothers Walt and Roy Disney set up the Disney Brothers Studio in Hollywood, California. Their first cartoon, Plane Crazy, directed by Walt Disney, was produced in 1928. The year 1937 marks a milestone in Disney History, because the studio produced its first animated feature film, Snow White and the Seven Dwarfs. Three years later, in 1940, the company went public and continued to produce other classic animation films such as Pinocchio and Fantasia. The first Disney Land Theme Park was opened in 1955, whereas Disney World Florida opened in 1971 and Disneyland Paris in 1992.

In the 1980s, Disney launched its first TV station – the Disney Channel – and also established the Disney MGM studio, later renamed the The Walt Disney Company. The year 1996 is another important year for the Disney Company, because it bought Capital Cities/ABC for $19 billion, which added 10 TV stations, 21 radio stations, 7 daily newspapers, and ownership positions in the cable networks A&E, Lifetime, History Channel and the sports network, ESPN, to their ever-growing business empire. In the second half of the 90s, Disney began buying into software and internet companies, which eventually went on to become their web portal The Walt Disney Internet Group.

During the first half of the 2000s, Disney entered multiple alliances with other companies like Kodak, Visa or Hewlett-Packard, offering them exclusive contracts and drawing upon joint marketing opportunities.

In the year 2003, Disney ended its partnership with the computer animation company Pixar, only to acquire it in 2006. Disney also added TV games developing companies to their portfolio and entered an agreement with Children's Place Retail Stores, who now operates the Disney Store retail chain in North America, comprising a total of 313 stores. In addition, in 2012 the company acquired Club Penguin, which is one of the fastest-growing online virtual worlds for kids.

Nowadays the Disney emporium consists of five business segments: media networks, parks and resorts, studio entertainment, consumer products, and interactive media. Its major products and services include:

Products:

- Television programs
- Motion pictures
- Plays
- Musical recordings
- Books
- Magazines
- Video games
- Mobile phones

Services:

- Entertainment program broadcasting
- Radio networks
- Radio stations
- Resorts
- Vacation club
- Cruise line
- Theme parks

Character-based merchandises:

- Toys
- Apparels
- Accessories
- Footwear
- Home furnishings
- Home decor
- Cosmetics

- Stationery
- Consumer electronics

Brands:

- Disney
- ABC
- ESPN

In the financial year 2011, The Walt Disney Company recorded revenues of $40.893 million, of which the media networks accounted for 45.8%. These figures serve to highlight the importance animated films and TV shows still have in the Disney emporium.

3.4.2. The Princess Franchise (see Disney Consumer Products Website)

Figure 7: Brand Logo of the Disney Princess Franchise

"Little girls never forget their first encounter with a Disney Princess. Even long after they're all grown up, they continue to pass along their love for these heroines, introducing them to their own daughters. Individual princesses have been part of the Disney scene since Snow White first graced the screen in 1937. However, only recently has Disney brought these beloved characters together in a collection of fantasy-based girls' entertainment and products – the Disney Princess brand." (Disney Consumer Products Homepage[7])

---

[7]   https://www.disneyconsumerproducts.com/Home/display.jsp?contentId=dcp_home_ourfranchises_ disney_princess_us&forPrint=false&language=en&preview=false&imageShow=0&pressRoom= US&translationOf=nul

To this point, the Disney Princess franchise comprises 10 heroines from 10 different Disney movies:

- Snow White from *Snow White and the Seven Dwarfs*
- Cinderella from *Cinderella*
- Aurora from *Sleeping Beauty*
- Ariel from *The Little Mermaid*
- Belle from *Beauty and the Beast*
- Jasmine from *Aladdin*
- Pocahontas from *Pocahontas*
- Mulan from *Mulan*
- Tiana from *The Princess and the Frog*
- Rapunzel from *Tangled*

Figure 8: Disney Princesses from left to right: Jasmine, Rapunzel, Snow White, Mulan, Aurora, Cinderella, Pocahontas, Tiana, Belle, Ariel; Source: http://images.wikia.com/disney/images/2/25/New-disney-princess-lineup-rapunzeldisney-princess-18212648-1280-800.jpg

Disney's strategy to support the Disney Princess brand year-round is not only through producing new animated movies, but also through offering affiliated consumer products, merchandise, theatrical releases, home videos, television, theme parks, a website, radio air play and live entertainment.

The target group of the Disney Princess franchise are young girls, starting at 2 years old. It is one of the fastest growing Disney Consumer Product brands with more than $4 billion in worldwide retail sales and $2.6 billion in box office revenues for Disney Princess animated films.

Its associated merchandise is the No. 1 girls' license toy brand in the United States among all girls and the No. 1 toy brand for dolls and role play among girls ages 2-5. Furthermore, the franchise has been ranked among the Top 10 most popular holiday gifts for the past five years, with more than 142 million books, 81 million sticker packs and 16 million Disney Princess magazines sold.

This goes to show how incredibly present and therefore influential Disney is in the lives of children nowadays. The movies do not only serve as entertainment, but rather turn children into consumers at a very early age. Seeing the popularity and success of the Disney Princess franchise, one can gather that young girls strive to be just like Cinderella or Pocahontas. Therefore, it is even more important to carefully study what role models these Disney Princesses (and their respective princes) are to children and what children take with them when watching Disney movies over and over again.

3.5. Gender & Ethnicity in Disney Movies

This chapter serves to give a brief overview over research already conducted within this particular field. I will use a study by Towbin et al. (2004) as a main structure and connect the findings of other authors and researchers accordingly.

In a 2004 study, Towbin et al. examine the portrayal of gender, race, age, and sexual orientation in a sample of 26 full-length animated Disney films[8]. They grouped their results according to 5 categories:*"(a) What it means to be a boy/man, (b) What it means to be a girl/woman, (c) What it means to be from a particular culture, (d) What it means*

---

[8] Snow White and the Seven Dwarfs, Pinocchio, Dumbo, Bambi, Cinderella, Alice in Wonderland, Peter Pan, Lady and the Tramp, Sleeping Beauty, 101 Dalmatians, The Sword in the Stone, The Jungle Book, Robin Hood, The Fox and the Hound, The Little Mermaid, The Rescuers Down Under, Beauty and the Beast, Aladdin, The Lion King, Pocahontas, The Hunchback of Notre Dame, Hercules, Mulan, Tarzan, Emperor's New Groove

to display characteristics of the opposite sex, and (e) What it means to be an older person". (Towbin et al., 2004, p. 28)

Taking a closer look at the depiction of male gender in the studied Disney movies, Towbin et al. (2004) list 5 themes which primarily emerged.

First, men primarily use physical force or means to express their emotions or they show no emotion at all. In nearly half of the movies, *"men and boys were more likely to respond to an emotional situation with physical, and in some cases, violent behaviour than through the use of words"* (Towbin et al., 2004, p. 28). At the same time, in some movies men were discouraged or not allowed to show any emotion at all. A very strong example for this is Shang, the main male character in the movie Mulan, who after finding his father's dead body *"immediately jumps on his horse to head into battle"* (Towbin et al., 2004, p. 29).

Another theme which emerged, was that men are naturally strong and heroic. Very often they are portrayed as the rescuers of the female characters and in the end they save the day. However, although men are shown as strong, they are not in control of their sexuality. Rather *"boys and men seemed to lose their senses in the presence of a beautiful woman".* What makes this observation even more troubling, is that in all the examples cited in the study, in the end the women got the blame for being so irresistible and tempting. (see Towbin et al., 2004, p. 28) Very often the men develop a sexual obsession for a woman, *"an obsession that puts the woman in direct physical danger"* (Bean, 2003, p. 62).

The fourth theme which emerged when analysing the depiction of men, was that men have non-domestic jobs. In 17 of the 26 movies, *"men were portrayed as having non-domestic jobs"* while *"[i]n only three movies [...] were men shown performing domestic tasks"* at all (Towbin et al., 2004, p. 28).

Lastly, overweight men are portrayed as being slow and unintelligent. Their depiction has a negative connotation as they are shown as being *"sloppy, unintelligent, and overly focused on eating"* (Towbin et al., 2004, p. 28).

While analysing the depiction of female characters in Disney movies, Towbin et al. (2004) observed four recurring themes, which were related to what it means to be a girl or a women.

Firstly, a woman's appearance is valued more than her intellect. This portrayal is especially apparent and typical in the first Disney movies (Snow White, Sleeping Beauty, Cinderella) and, ironically, is especially visible in *Beauty and the Beast.* (see Towbin et al, 2004, p. 30) At the time of release of the movie *Beauty and the Beast*, Disney announced Belle as the most feminist Disney Princess to date, owing to the fact that Belle loves to read and is portrayed as independent[9]. However, within the first five minutes of the movie, *"[h]er beauty is celebrated [...] but her intellect ridiculed"*. Although in later movies, girls and women were also valued for their accomplishments, in most movies, at some point their beauty and their looks outweighed their accomplishments and their skills. (see Towbin et al, 2004, p. 30)

In a study analyzing the so-called "what-is-beautiful-is-good" stereotype Bazinni et al., (2010, p. 2706-2707) came to the conclusion that *"[t]aken together, the current investigations empirically support the anecdotal observations that animated Disney movies promote the stereotype that what is beautiful is good. Indeed, in some Disney films, attractive characters are portrayed as being more morally virtuous and less aggressive, and as achieving more positive life outcomes than unattractive characters"*.

Another observation was that women are helpless and in need of protection. This goes hand in hand with the fact that men are often portrayed as the rescuers. Towbin et al. do concede the point that in newer movies girls and women are also portrayed as independent and adventurous, but in most cases, in the end they still needed to be rescued by the male hero. (see Towbin et al., 2004, p. 31)

Brenda Ayres (2003, p. 39) argues that this is to be expected, as Disney often adapts Victorian tales. In these tales, *"[w]omen are to be submissive, self-denying, modest, childlike, innocent, industrious, maternal, and angelic [...]. They are descriptors in con-*

---

[9] http://disney.wikia.com/wiki/Belle

*trast to men, who are their own nominatives. Men are the explorers, inventors, and ne-
gotiators of the world 'out there'"*.

Thirdly, the study showed that women are more domestic and likely to marry. While in
only 3 movies out of 26, men were shown performing domestic tasks, women were
shown in domestic roles in 17 out of 26 movies. On top of that, *"[only] in two movies
was marriage not seen as the ultimate goal for women"* (Towbin et al., 2004, p. 31).

Christine Yzaguirre (2006, p. 48) argues that Disney heroines have evolved in the past
years and newer heroines do not comply as much as older ones. She calculated the time
women were shown on camera performing household chores and time spent acting
against societal expectations. She came to the result that older heroines spend an average of 2.57% of the time performing household chores, while newer heroines spend an
average of 0.25% of their film time doing chores. And while the older Disney Princesses spend no time at all rebelling against societal norms and conventions, newer Disney
Princesses spent an average of 12.36% of time *"acting against what is expected of
them"*[10].

However, compared to the male heroes not doing any domestic chores at all (see
above), it stands to say that women are *still* being depicted doing household chores.
This fact is important to consider as Connell (2001, p. 51) asserts that *"[b]odies as
agents in social practice are involved in the very construction of the social world, the
bringing-into-being of social reality. The social world is never simply reproduced. It is
always reconstituted by practice."* Put differently, the ongoing depiction of Disney heroines continuously performing household chores (although not as much) while Disney
heroes do not, is constantly validating outdated gender roles.

Lastly, Towbin et al. observed that overweight women are portrayed as being ugly, unpleasant, and unmarried. (see Towbin et al., 2004, p. 31)

---

[10] Yzaguirre's study does not include the latest two movies *The Princess and the Frog* and *Rapunzel*. As
those two princesses in particular spend a lot of time doing chores and working, I do believe that the percentage for the newer heroines might be a bit higher at this point in time.

Upon closer analysis of the representation of non-dominant cultures, five themes emerged: (a) negative representations of non-dominant cultures; (b) exaggerated class stereotypes; (c) only Western values and Christianity depicted; (d) characters who share similar values should stay/be together; and (e) characters who share different values can be friends and create community together. (see Towbin et al., 2004, p. 31-32)

A very important observation was that in many movies only western values and Christianity were depicted. Often, nearly all characters were white and only themes from the dominant culture were portrayed. On top of this *"the expectation was that all people are or should be like this"*. Non-western beliefs were only present in four of the movies. (see Towbin et al., 2004, p. 33)

Due to the fact that the people in Disney movies are animated, it is important to critically analyze the depiction of other races in those movies. Dotsch (2001, p. 978-980) shows in a study that ethnic faces are biased in the prejudiced mind. He proposes *"that prejudice [...] biases the way people conceptualize the facial appearance of outgroup members"*. As popular belief links personality traits of a person to their facial features, he tests if *"prejudiced people also have more negatively stereotyped mental representations of ethnic faces than less prejudiced people"*. He comes to the result that *"people's representations of ethnic faces are related to their level of prejudice"* and that *"[t]he present results have important implications for whom people identify as members of stigmatized groups"*.

This is important to know, because in the case of Disney movies, this could mean that the personal prejudice an animator or maybe even several people working on a movie hold, can influence their depiction of other ethnicities in Disney movies. Lee Artz (2004, p. 118) argues that *"[a]nimation has considerably more representational latitude than non-animated film: Image, size, movement, colour, lighting and continuity are easily altered with the stroke of a pen or key. [...] [A]nimated characters, settings, and representations can be graphically adjusted to empower desired meanings."*

The study of Towbin et al. (2004) further showed that when other races and cultures were present in the movies, non-dominant cultures were often portrayed negatively. The negative stereotyping is not limited to only one race or ethnicity, but rather encompasses the depiction of any kind of non-dominant (and in Disney's case this means non-white) culture. Ethnicities which were shown in a negative light were (among others) Afro-Americans, Chinese, Hispanics, Middle Easterners, Native Americans or Gypsies. In most cases, these negative portrayals concerned people, however, the study does show that sometimes other cultures and habits (as in setting, tradition, habits, dress, architecture) are shown accurately or even positively. (see Towbin et al., 2004, p. 32)

Two further themes which emerged seem to have contradictory tendencies. On the one hand, in some movies there was the overall tenor that *"characters must share the same values in order to get along"*. On the other hand, in other movies the overall message was that *"different types of characters can get along and create [a] community"* (Towbin et al, 2004, p. 33). [11]

Lastly, the study also showed that *"class stereotypes are exaggerated"*. This means that movies often present hierarchical structures, which either show the lower class as poor or stupid or as enjoying serving the rich. (see Towbin et al., 2004, p. 32-33)

Two further topics of analysis were the dimensions of sexual orientation and age. Towbin et al. observed an *"absence of gay characters–portrayal"* and a primarily negative depiction of opposite-gender behaviour. Also, the typical characteristics of older people were mostly negative. Elderly people are very often portrayed as being forgetful, stupid, easily flustered, crotchety, grump, mean, short-tempered, or ugly. Only three movies include positive portrayals of older people. (see Towbin et al., 2004, p. 33-35)

Overall, they conclude that *"[a]lthough some positive changes have occurred in Disney films over time, many of the messages remain the same or are mixed"* (Towbin et al., 2004, p. 35). Their findings confirm once more, what previous studies have attested: *"Gender stereotypes continue to be portrayed, and non-dominant groups are portrayed negatively, marginalized, or not portrayed at all"* (Towbin et al., 2004, p. 35).

---

[11] This may seem contradictory at first, but being familiar with the contents of the films analysed, can be partly explained when taking a closer look at the movies Towbin et al. listed as examples for both themes. While the first case "characters must share the same values in order to get along" often describes situations, where a main character is forced to decide between their families respectively his or her people and their romantic interest, in the second scenario "different types of characters can get along and create [a] community" relates to movies, where the main characters have no or a non-traditional family and therefore the community substitutes the core-family.

3.6. Adapting the fairy tales

When it comes to reviewing the Disney films, one has to keep in mind that in most cases, the stories presented are not original. In case of the ten movies of the Disney Princess franchise, most of them are based on fairy tales or myths.[12] However, Disney does not only adapt those stories to be suitable as movies, but very often takes liberties in interpreting them (and their moral) and also has a long-standing habit of changing key facts. The following chapter will give a few examples to illustrate this point.

In their study, Towbin et al. (2004) come to the conclusion that *"one of the most disturbing facets of Disney movies is the way in which stories are reinterpreted"*. This may be disconcerting in two ways. Firstly, Disney often chooses to retell stories in a way, so they fit into the dominant social paradigm and therefore often disregard the story's original moral message. Secondly, several times Disney has even rewritten history itself in inaccurate ways. (see Towbin et al., 2004, p. 39)

In the original tale of *Snow White* the queen tries to kill Snow White three times, whereas in the movie she only tries once. However, this is a rather insignificant change compared to the fact that in the original fairy tale the prince never kisses Snow White. Rather, his servants stumble while carrying the glass coffin, which dislodges the piece of poisoned apple stuck in Snow White's throat. (see Ayres, 2003, p. 46) Put differently, Disney *invented* the *kiss of true love*.

In Hans Christian Andersen's tale of *The Little Mermaid* the characters live in a female-dominated world in which the king is barely even mentioned. The mermaids serve as supporting network for the heroine and are sources of inspiration and independence. The grandmother of the little mermaid plays a central role, as she tells all the enticing stories of the human world. (see Sorracco, 1990, p. 409, as cited in Finkelstein, 2003, p. 134) She is the *"principal parent and figure of authority"* (Ingwersen & Ingwersen, 1990, p. 415, as cited in Finkelstein, 2003, p. 137).

However, Disney turns this matriarchal society in a patriarchal society. The most significant change to signify this is by omitting the character of the grandmother, therefore

---

[12] List of sources https://en.wikipedia.org/wiki/List_of_sources_for_Disney_theatrical_animated_features

"the film shows only the negative side of female rule" (Ingwersen & Ingwersen, 1990, p. 415 as cited in Finkelstein, 2003, p. 137). In exchange, the role of the father Triton, who is even given a name (as opposed to the narrative), is broadly expanded. Ursula, the sea witch, is explicitly put in the position of Triton's enemy, *"an opposition absent from Andersen"*. (see Finkelstein, 2003, p. 134) Also, the happy ending as shown in the Disney movie, does not occur in the book. Rather, the prince chooses not to marry the little mermaid. He states many times *"that he wishes she could speak to him"*, but as she could not the prince married another woman (see Towbin et al., 2004, p. 39) and *"Andersen's mermaid [gained] the hope of salvation through three hundred years of work after sacrificing[13] herself"* (Finkelstein, 2003, p. 134).

Also, in *Mulan* the film presents a so-called matchmaker, who assesses young girls and decides whether they can be married or not. Towbin et al. (2004, p. 39) note that *"[h]istorically, there was no such behaviour in China; the culture is represented as far more sexist and oppressive than it actually was"*.

Another example is *Pocahontas*, where *"history is rewritten as to be unrecognizable"* (Chyng 2001, as cited in Towbin et al., 2004, p. 39). Although there was a Native American named Pocahontas who saved an Englishman named John Smith from being killed, they were never romantically involved with each other. In real life, Pocahontas was still a child when she met John Smith. (see Towbin et al., 2004, p. 39)

However, the most blatant change is the fact that in the movie Pocahontas, the English settlers return to England after Pocahontas prevented the war. As history shows, the European settlers stayed in America and as opposed to leaving, more and more arrived. Eventually, *"in a massive act of genocide"* the new settlers killed nearly all of the Native Americans. (see Towbin et al., 2004, p. 39)

Lastly, while in the movie Pocahontas decides to stay with her people and not going with her love John Smith, the real Pocahontas eventually married an Englishman and went to England, where she soon died of illness. (see Towbin et al., 2004, p. 39)

---

[13] In the original tale, the mermaid is offered to regain her original form by killing the prince. She refuses and as his marriage to another woman signifies her death, she is sacrificing herself for the prince. http://www.alkotagifts.com/fairytales/little_mermaid.php

In the context of Disney retelling old fairy tales and folks stories, there is also the matter of why a 21st century institution would choose to retell stories which bear the moral codes and gender-roles of social structures long passed. In other words, the *choice* of source material for Disney movies can be questioned as well (and not only Disney's liberal style at adapting them). *"That Disney mirrors a Victorian tale is so to say that Disney also perpetuates a nineteenth century notion of domestic ideology. [...] The purpose of both Grimms' and Disney's fairy tales is to frame females into a patriarchally acceptable portrait of a womanly ideal."* (Ayres, 2003, p. 39-40)

As stated above, Disney takes great liberties when it comes to adapting its source material. However, using *Snow White* as an example, Ayres (2003, p. 45) points out that *"Disney's film animation adopts these (author's note: Victorian) ideological codes even though it deviates from the fairy tale in significant ways"*. This does raise the question of a possible hidden agenda, as the changes made very seemingly serve to present or strengthen outdated patriarchal settings in which traditional gender-roles and family settings are portrayed an (re)-produced. *"The Disney film thus is not desecrating a purer, more appealing version, but is part of a system which creates 'ideals' [...] using an earlier fictional system which did the same."* (Finkelstein, 2003, p. 132)

This chapter serves to underline the fact that the gender and racial ideologies discussed later on in the analysis, are not simply a product of Disney retelling stories which are several centuries old, but rather a conscious and deliberate decision (and a business model) on Disney's part.

4. Critical Discourse Analysis

In order to ensure an in-depth and comprehensive analysis of the films, I have chosen to use the Critical Discourse Analysis based on the work of Siegfried Jäger (2009). Jäger is a German linguist, who further developed the Critical Discourse Analysis based on the works of Michel Foucault and Jürgen Link.

Critical Discourse Analysis (CDA) is originally a tool used for linguistic text analysis; however, it strives to broaden the concept of text. Its goal is not only to analyse written text word for word, but rather to analyze the meaning and impact of these written documents within society as a whole. Therefore, the analysis of discourse and text is seen as a method pertaining to cultural sciences rather than linguistics. (see Jäger 2009)

The above raises the question, why I use Critical Discourse Analysis as my method to analyse films, when it was originally designed to analyse text. To answer this I will take a small detour and go a bit further in-depth in explaining Critical Discourse Analysis.

Jäger starts to explain text in the following way: *"The product of speaking is initially text; its social function (put in a very general way) consists in enabling people to verbalise a thought, in order to make it receivable for others (or in some cases for themselves, i.e. at a later point in time)"*[14] (Jäger, 2009, p. 113).

When it comes to movies, we can turn his argument around and say: The produced dialogue was initially text. Moreover, not only the dialogues, but rather the whole movie was originally a written script, translated into frames and dialogue. Therefore, movies can also be seen as visualised text. When we are talking about Disney films, the above drafted train of thoughts does not seem farfetched either, seeing how many Disney movies are based on written books of fairy tales, myths or ancient legends.

Also, over the course of the past decades, Critical Discourse Analysis has started to attract considerable interest and attention outside of linguistics and language studies. Critical Discourse Analysis has since been used in various fields of the social sciences or

---

[14] Translated by author

humanities, e.g. Sociology, Cultural Studies, Gender Studies, Media Studies, Politics or History. (see Fairclough, 2001)

Van Dijk (2001, p. 352) depicts that *"[c]ritical discourse analysis is a type of discourse analytical research that primarily studies the way social power abuse, dominance, and inequality are enacted, reproduced, and resisted by text and talk in the social and political context"*.

When using Critical Discourse Analysis as a tool to analyze (different) media, one assumes that (mass) media has a decisive influence on the formation of a subject. Put differently, mass media has a lot of authority not only on consumers' construction of their environment, but also helps creating their self-perception. (see Jäger, 2009)

Fairclough (2001, p. 41-42) discusses this inequality in power in a segment called „hidden power". He concedes the point that a considerable portion of discourse within society is indirect and involves mass media (television, radio, films, newspapers). He points out that the special interest within mass media discourse lies in the "*hidden relations of power*". Due to separation of time and place of the participants in the discourse, the "*nature of the power relations enacted in it is often not clear*". Due to this one-sidedness in media discourse, the participants are no longer both producer and interpreter of text, but rather turn into producer and 'consumer' with the media 'product' being an exchanged commodity between them. Seeing how these media products are being produced for large audiences, the producer can no longer adapt and respond to unique persons or diverse sections within that audience. Fairclough points out that *"[...] since all discourse producers must produce with some interpreters in mind, what media producers do is address an ideal subject, be it viewer, or listener, or reader."* Considering this information, one can easily deduct that discourse producers in mass media are in a rather comfortable position, from where they can exercise power over the consumer and decide on what and who is included and excluded in the discourse.

Van Dijk (2001, p. 356) further explains that if "*discourse is defined in terms of complex communicative events, access and control may be defined both for the* context *and for the* structure of text and talk themselves. " Hence, it is not only control over the discourse itself, but more specifically control over a greater portion and more influential discourse (and discourse properties) which equal to greater power and higher influence.

Jäger (2009) argues in a similar way. Although he starts out by explaining text, he also asserts that one has to separate the impact of text and its discursive impact respectively. While the impression a piece of text has on its own is minimal, the impressions of discursive outputs are rather sustainable. This is achieved by the permanent recurrence of subject matters, symbols, and strategies, which in the course of time form and solidify "knowledge". He generally defines discourse as a *"river of 'knowledge' through time"* (Jäger, 2009, p. 129) and therefore, discourse has always been more or less structured and fixed (in terms of social convention). As a result, discourse can also be seen as an *'transmitter of (currently valid) knowledge"* (Jäger, 2009, p. 149). In this function of bearing knowledge, discourses not only have the authority to exert power, they themselves are instruments of power in their own right, by being able to elicit certain behavioural responses or induce other discourses.

Jäger (2009) further reasons that, since this (hegemonic and therefore temporary) 'knowledge' is considered to be *true* knowledge and is reinforced as such in sciences and everyday life respectively, discourse helps in shaping and structuring the hierarchy and distribution of power within a society. He proposes that Critical Discourse Analysis offers the possibility to scrutinize this 'knowledge' in a critical manner and to challenge its supporting institutions and rules.

5. Methodology

Considering the above presented information, two facts have to be established. First, Disney is a company and as such, operates to its business' best interest. Second, Disney is one of the most powerful, if not *the* most powerful force in the children's entertainment segment. Therefore, we can assume that not only does Disney participate in the social discourse geared towards children, but rather that it is the driving force behind it. Consequently, as such a "'producer' of discourse, it has an enormous influence on the socialization of our children and on their perception of their environment. Therefore the Critical Discourse Analysis seemed to be the appropriate tool to analyze the Disney movies.

Jäger developed his analysis framework with text in mind. Therefore, I adapted his model slightly so it can be applied to analysing movies as well. There are five main points, which need to be considered in the analyses (see Jäger 2009, p. 183):[15]

- *Institutional framework:* Every fragment of the discourse belongs to an institutional context. This, amongst others, includes the medium, the creator, possible occurrences which correlate to this fragment, or a certain motive for the creation of this fragment.

- *"Surface":* Applied to films, surface means the visual creation of characters and their environment. How do they look? What do they wear? How do they move and interact?

- *Linguistical and rhetorical devices:* This part of the framework highlights the need to listen closer to idioms used. How do characters talk? Which metaphors are used? Which style and register of language is used? In this context, this also includes accents or ethnically coded language. What kind of arguments and references are used?

- *Ideological messages with regards to content:* Which "idea of man" is postulated? What is the presented concept of society? To what kind of future does it allude?

---

[15] Translated by author

- *Interpretation:* Steps one to four serve as preparation for the analysis and the interpretation of the reviewed material. When analyzing and interpreting the films, these different aspects have to be connected and be brought together, to form a complete picture.

Based on this framework, I developed two tables. The first one is a general one, helping with the overall assessment of the movies and laying the groundwork for the actual review of the individual movies. The second grid was developed using parts of the first grid and served as a checklist when watching the films.

In the analysis and discussions of my findings, the separate points from the grid will not be dealt with individually. As Jäger suggested, my previous readings, my observations and my findings have been put together to find common and recurring themes within the movies, which serve to reproduce stereotypes. I have decided to group my analysis into these themes rather than discuss each movie individually, in order to facilitate the understanding and at the same time highlight the formulaic and systematic design of the films discussed.

General	Film		Characters				Reviews
	General	*Content*	*Visualisation*	*Language*	*Behaviour / Demeanour*	*Additional info*	*Interpretation & Analysis*
• Political & medial occurences • Gender and Diversity discourse respectively • Other important public occurrences?	• Year of release • (Financial) Success?	• Summary of film • Underlying fairy tale, myth, legend	• Bodies • Clothing • Ethnicity, Skin colour • Body language	• Language • Dialects, slangs, ethnically coded language • Metaphors • Lyrics	• Disposition / Temper • Tics, Quirks • Development • Important, relevant decisions	• Role → What is their purpose? • Means to an end? • Upgrading main character?	• Reviews of the movies • Critical review and analysis → Literature review

Table 1: General grid for the analysis of the reviewed movies; incorporates the general themes which will be analysed; used as a guideline to develop the second grid

MOVIE: (Title of the Movie)

General	
Name	
Sex	
Age	
Skin colour, Ethnicity	
Visualisation	
Body, Design	
Clothing, attire	
Language	
Manner of speaking	
Dialects, Slangs, Metaphors	
Behaviour, comportment	
Characteristics, disposition, temper	
Body language	
Tics, Quirks	
Development	
Important / relevant deeds and decisions	
Other Information	
Lyrics	
Additional Info	

Table 2: Check-list used during review of the movies

I decided to limit my analysis to the films encompassed in the so-called Disney Princess franchise. This, as well as the limitation to gender and ethnic/racial stereotypes, serves the manageability and comparability of the findings discussed on the following pages.

6. Film Analysis & Discussion

In this chapter I will present the findings of my analysis. Before I start with the analysis, there will be a short overview of the movies in question. In the first part of the analysis itself I will focus on gender stereotypes found in Disney Princess movies, while the second part will deal primarily with ethnic and racial stereotypes.

6.1. Overview of Movies

First, I want to give a few key facts of the movies reviewed and name the characters (main characters or side characters) used for the analysis in order to facilitate the understanding, especially for readers not as familiar with Disney movies and characters. If not otherwise indicated, the information was taken from "The Disney Wiki", (see http://disney.wikia.com/).

- **Snow White and the Seven Dwarfs**

Year of Release:	1937
Budget:	$1,488,000 (est.)
Gross Revenue:	$184,925,486 (domestic)[16]
(Main) Characters:	Snow White
	The Stepmother (antagonist)
	The Seven Dwarfs
	The Prince
Additional Info:	The world's first full-length animated feature.

- **Cinderella**

Year of Release:	1950
Budget:	$2,900,000
Gross Revenue:	$85,000,000
(Main) Characters:	Cinderella
	The Stepmother and Stepsisters (antagonists)
	Prince Charming
	The King and his advisor

---

[16] retrieved from http://www.boxofficemojo.com/movies/?id=snowwhite.htm [28.02.2012; 21:20]

Additional Info:　　　　Cinderella is Disney's most popular and iconic Disney Prin-
　　　　　　　　　　　cess, as well as the most celebrated Disney movie of all time.

- **Sleeping Beauty**

  Year of Release:　　　1959
  Budget:　　　　　　$8,500,000
  Financial Success:　　$36,479,805 (domestic)[17]
  (Main) Characters:　　Aurora
  　　　　　　　　　　The three good fairies
  　　　　　　　　　　Maleficent (antagonist)
  　　　　　　　　　　Prince Philipp
  　　　　　　　　　　The King and the Queen (Aurora's parents)
  Additional Info:　　　Upon first release, *Sleeping Beauty* returned only half of the
  　　　　　　　　　　invested sum, nearly bankrupting the Disney studio, however,
  　　　　　　　　　　the film has gained a following since then and is today hailed
  　　　　　　　　　　as one of the best animated features ever made.

- **The Little Mermaid**

  Year of Release:　　　1989
  Budget:　　　　　　$40,000,000
  Gross Revenue:　　　$211,343,479
  (Main) Characters:　　Ariel
  　　　　　　　　　　Ursula (antagonist)
  　　　　　　　　　　Triton
  　　　　　　　　　　Prince Eric
  　　　　　　　　　　Sebastian (crab)
  Additional Info:　　　*The Little Mermaid* is the first movie to be again based upon
  　　　　　　　　　　a fairy tale after *Sleeping Beauty*. With a U.S. grossing of
  　　　　　　　　　　$111 million and an additional $99 million worldwide it is
  　　　　　　　　　　given credit for breathing life back into the animated feature
  　　　　　　　　　　film genre after a string of critical and commercial failures
  　　　　　　　　　　beginning in the early 1980s.

---

[17] retrieved from http://www.boxofficemojo.com/movies/?id=sleepingbeauty.htm [28.02.2012; 21:30]

- **Beauty and the Beast**

Year of Release:	1991
Budget:	$25,000,000
Gross Revenue:	$377,350,553
(Main) Characters:	Belle
	Beast / Prince
	Gaston (antagonist)
	Maurice (Belle's father)
Additional Info:	The movie *Beauty and the Beast* was nominated for several awards, and won the Golden Globe Award for Best Motion Picture - Musical or Comedy (for the first time to an animated movie). Additionally, *Beauty and the Beast* was the first ever (and until 2009 only) animated film to be nominated for the Academy Award for Best Picture.

- **Aladdin**

Year of Release:	1992
Budget:	$28,000,000
Gross Revenue:	$781,000,000 ($869,631,000 adj)
(Main) Characters:	Aladdin
	Jasmine
	Jafar (antagonist)
	Sultan (Jasmine's father)
Additional Info:	It was the (financially) most successful film of 1992.[18]

- **Pocahontas**

Year of Release:	1995
Budget:	$55,000,000 (est)
Gross Revenue:	$346,079,773[19]

---

[18] From 2 August 1990 to 28 February 1991 the Gulf War took place. Dianne Macleod (2003) argues that the *"televised staging of the Gulf War"* contributed greatly to *Aladdin's* success, as *"mirroring and magnifying popular stereotypes of Arab culture,* Aladdin *played to an audience already primed by the media"*. (Macleod, 2003, p. 179)

[19] retrieved from www.boxofficemojo.com/movies/?id=pocahontas.htm [28.02.2012; 22:00]

(Main) Characters:	Pocahontas
	John Smith
	Kocoum
	Radcliffe (antagonist)
	Chief (Pocahonta's father)
Additional Info:	Story based on a real historic character.

- **Mulan**

Year of Release:	1998
Budget:	$70,000,000
Gross Revenue:	$424,000,00
(Main) Characters:	Mulan
	Shang
	Shan Yu (antagonist)
	The Huns (antagonists)
	Matchmaker

Additional Info: Disney hoped the movie would help restore relations with the Chinese government which threatened to curtail business negotiations after the release of *Kundun*, a Disney-funded biography of the Dalai Lama that the Chinese government considered politically provocative. There was a limited Chinese release after a year's delay.

- **The Princess and The Frog**

Year of Release:	2009
Budget:	$105,000,000
Gross Revenue:	$269,312,336
(Main) Characters:	Tiana
	Prince Naveen
	Dr. Facilier (antagonist)

Additional Info: First African-American Disney Princess. The working title of the movie was *The Frog Princess*, which raised some criticism already in advance of the release.

- **Tangled**

Year of Release:	2010
Budget:	$260,000,000
Gross Revenue:	$590,721,936
(Main) Characters:	Rapunzel
	Flynn Rider / Eugene Fitzherbert
	Gothel (antagonist, Rapunzel's „stepmother")
	The King and the Queen (Rapunzel's parents)
Additional Info:	Disney was criticized for altering the classic title (and story) from *Rapunzel* to *Tangled* as a marketing strategy, in order to market the film to both boys and girls.

This overview should help navigate through the analysis. As already explained above, I have decided to group my findings into recurring themes, which can be found through-out the movies. These sub-topics can be found in various intensities and will show that although at first glance it seems great changes have been made, there actually has not really been a lot of progress when it comes to gender and ethnic depiction in Disney Princess movies.

6.2. Gender Stereotypes

As the analysis and discussion of the films will show, the Disney Princess movies work with a lot of gender based stereotypes, both for women and for men. This work will primarily focus on gender stereotypes geared towards women, since I believe them to have a greater negative impact, however, some stereotypes aimed towards men will be discussed rudimentarily as well.

6.2.1. True (heterosexual) Love

First, it has to be established that all love stories in these movies promote a heterosexual normativity. For the first three princesses, finding true and romantic love are the prima-ry goals. They do not pursue any other interests but finding "the one" and the whole film is geared towards overcoming the obstacles to finally get to "the kiss of true love". Later Disney Princess movies do not primarily focus on their heroines finding true love, but give them other goals to pursue first. However, during the course of the movie, these other goals slowly get pushed to the background as the (fulfilment) of the love story takes centre place. What also can be noted as a common thread in the movies, is that "finding love" very often serves as an escape route or as a means to satisfy the heroines' longing for more.

Snow White knows her true love even before she ever met him. In the beginning of the movie, we see her cleaning the castle while singing *"I'm wishing, for the one I love, to find me today. I'm hoping, and I'm dreaming, of the nice things he'll say"*. So not only is Snow White's only goal in life to meet her true love, but on top of that she has to passively wait for her love to find her and does not actively seek out love herself. One can also quickly gather that for her love to find her, is Snow White's expression of her wish to flee the life under the rule of her stepmother. Her prince will take her away, say nice things to her and her life will better right away. To prove that he actually is her true love, Disney even changed the original fairy tale to include the famous kiss. While in the original Snow White wakes up because the piece of apple which was stuck in her throat got dislodged, in the Disney movie it is the prince's kiss of true love which saves her life. (see Ayres, 2003, p. 44)

Figure 9: Snow White and the Prince, Source :http://disney.wikia.com/wiki/ File:S-16_SnowWhite2.png

The same goes for Cinderella, who does not know "her love" yet, but believes if she keeps on wishing, her dreams will come true and her heartache will go away. While singing this song she longingly looks at the castle in the distance, telling the audience without words that her wish is to be married to the prince. But even before Cinderella begins to sing herself, the lyrics of the opening song tell us right away that Cinderella should not be a servant, that she is actually (socially) equal to the prince and that love will save her.

> *Cinderella, you're as lovely as your name. / Cinderella, you're a sunset in a frame.*
> *Though you're dressed in rags, you wear an air of queenly grace. / Anyone can see a throne would be your proper place.*
> *Cinderella, if you give your heart a chance, it will lead you to the kingdom of romance. / There you see your dreams unfold.*

Figure 10: Cinderella and Prince Charming
Source: http://disney.wikia.com/ wiki/File:Dibujo203.1.jpg

And indeed, Prince Charming falls in love with her at first sight and in the end marries her and the "kingdom of romance" saves her from her horrible life with her stepmother and stepsisters.

Aurora faces the same dilemma as did Snow White and Cinderella. Locked away in an isolated cabin in the woods, she longs for someone to take her away and show her the world. This princess as well tells us through song that she "*want[s] to sing love songs to somebody*", she "*wonder[s] when she will be found [...] for true love conquers all*". Luckily for her, Prince Philipp chooses that particular moment to ride by and instantly falls in love with her. And again, in the end, the "kiss of true love" bestowed upon Aurora by Prince Philipp breaks Maleficent's curse and saves Aurora (and the whole kingdom).

Thirty years later, Ariel, the heroine from *The Little Mermaid*, does not actively seek for love in the beginning of the movie. Rather, she "*want[s] more*", she wants to be "*part of that world*". After all, "*bright young women [are] sick of swimming*". However, after seeing and saving Prince Eric, her wish to be "*part of* that *world*" quickly turns into being "*part of* your *world*". She is unhappy undersea and finding love with her prince would mean she could flee this unhappiness.

Jasmine, the princess in Aladdin, is unhappy as well. She has never in her life left the palace and feels caged. Now she must choose a prince to marry, because the law says so. So when Aladdin comes along and takes her on a magic carpet ride to "*show her a whole new world*", Jasmine accepts too gladly. And since Jasmine and Aladdin truly love each other, the Sultan decides to change the law so Jasmine can be with whomever she deems worthy. Once again, true love conquers all and helps our heroine escape her miserable life.

Sadly, it seems this concept still works in 2010. In the latest Disney Princess movie *Tangled*, we once again find our heroine Rapunzel locked away in a tower, longing for more. And although it certainly is not love at first sight when it comes to Flynn Rider, ultimately it is the love between them which motivates Flynn to save her and which gets her out of the tower and back to her family.

Disney clearly postulates the idea of "one true love which conquers all" and which leads to a happily ever after. And to make matters worse, they not only promote an ideal which is rarely found in real life, but every other feat which our heroines might achieve means nothing, when it does not lead them to romance as well. Examples for this can be found in two later Princess movies, *Mulan* and *The Princess and the Frog*.

Mulan takes her father's place in the army to help him and ends up defeating the Huns and saving the emperor of China. As a reward she not only receives the imperial seal, the sword of the defeated leader of the Huns, and gets offered a very prestigious position in court, but the emperor (and in consequence all of China) even bows to her. However, all of these things seem of little valour to her when Shang, her love interest, does not immediately confess his feelings to her.

In a slightly different setting, we see Tiana (*The Princess and the Frog*) working hard to fulfil her dreams of owning a restaurant. Yet, instead of supporting her, her mother tells her that she works too hard and that she should settle down, because she *"want[s] to have grandchildren"*. She also reveals to her that while her father may not have had everything, *"he still had love"*. Eventually we see Tiana ready to sacrifice all her dreams to be with Prince Naveen, choosing love over her own restaurant.

While Mulan and Tiana do get *both* in the end, their rewards respectively their restaurant *and* the romance, the movies still convey the message that if you have to choose of the two, love and a romantic relationship should be put above everything else. Consequently, a woman who maybe is successful in her job or otherwise (politics, sports, etc.) will still be unhappy and unsatisfied as long as she does not have romance in her life. On the other hand, romance is always a sure way to lead a happy and satisfied life. It is very clear that Disney promotes ideas and ideals of love, which may lead to unrealistic expectations in children.

6.2.2. Families, Mothers & Fathers

The above discussed idea of love in the Disney Princess movies should not stand on its own. It has to be linked to the idealized vision of the nuclear family, meaning a family consisting of a mother, a father and a child. Once we broaden the focus on (heterosexual) romance and love and include the portrayed image of family it becomes clear very quickly that Disney has a whole other agenda at hand in following these love centric storylines. What Disney does, is idealising the stereotypical traditional family and promoting very conservative role-models of men and women, which paint the women as soft and warm and assign them the responsibility for housekeeping while the men are the protectors and providers.

Disney was and still is clearly associated with family and family entertainment. Therefore, it comes as a surprise that a lot of Disney heroines suffer the fate of being motherless (Snow White, Ariel, Pocahontas, Jasmine), in some cases even being complete orphans left in the care of some evil stepmother (Cinderella). In his essay "Beauties and Their Beasts & Other Motherless tales from the Wonderful World of Walt Disney", Axelrod (2003, p. 29) asks how Disney can maintain this image, when *"some of Disney's greatest animated achievements are, if not misogynistic, works that have devalued motherhood and the role of the mother within the nuclear family"*? He illustrates three ways in which Disney tends to deal with matronly and/or womanly figures:

- the role of the mother is utterly neglected or completely eliminated
- the role of the mother is being replaced with an evil, cruel stepmother
- the leading female authority figure is neither a mother nor a stepmother, but rather a power hungry, evil character

Finally, he comes to the conclusion that *"[f]or over five decades (if not longer) it (author's note: Disney) has been able to maintain the image of a family-oriented family company (albeit transnational), while at the same time producing a product that if not demeaning to mothers, then totally ignores them in the grand scheme of child rearing and in the extended name of "family values"* (Axelrod, 2003, p. 37).

I disagree with Axelrod's findings. On the contrary, I believe that by omitting the mothers or reconstituting them as evil stepmothers Disney seeks to underline the importance of mothers being present in the life of a child and reinforces the notion that without a mother, fathers and children alike are lost and will succumb to total chaos. In order to emphasise this point further, Disney creates father figures which:

- die very early in the film (*Cinderella, The Princess and the Frog*)
- are absent in the life of their children (*Snow White and the Seven Dwarfs*)
- are completely clumsy, idiotic and behave like children themselves (*Sleeping Beauty, Cinderella, Beauty and the Beast, Aladdin*)
- are very proud and caught in stereotypical male behaviour and therefore, although they are loving fathers, cannot communicate properly with their children and drive them away (*The Little Mermaid, Mulan, Pocahontas*)
- are completely powerless to help and protect their children and are therefore neglected in the storyline (*Sleeping Beauty, Tangled*)

Ayres and Hines (2003, p. 6) point out that "*[...] Disney's animated films tend to focus on the absence or dissolution of families. While courting family viewer empathy, the Disney impetus is to confirm status quo family values by depicting most nontraditional families, most nonnuclear families, as painfully lacking or wholly dysfunctional. The message is clear: In traditional families, threats are always external. [...] Nontraditional families, however, are usually plagued with internal, domestic troubles.*"

Including above listed points, I argue that the heroines in Disney Princess movies do not fall in love with the princes only for love and romance's sake, but rather to be able to start their own families and be mothers. Put differently, the (fulfilled) love story is not the end, but rather the means to the end. It serves as a vehicle to enable the heroines to leave their homes and be wives and mothers themselves, fulfilling the stereotypical gender-role assigned to them.

This desire to have their own perfect families is fuelled and strengthened by having imperfect families or weak parents. Left without parental guidance, the heroines have to become a parent themselves to restore order and peace. Additionally, in order to accomplish this, it is the heroines who have to leave their lives and families of origin behind or as Snow White sings "*[a]way to his castle we go, to be happy forever I know*".

In order to give further prove for this assumption, I would like to show some further in-depth analysis of some of the movies.

In *Snow White*, we only get to see Snow White's evil stepmother. This could lead to the assumption that both of her parents are dead and Snow White is actually an orphan. However, it is only said that Snow White's mother died, which means her father is still alive and present, just not in Snow White's life. What kind of father would submit his own daughter to the kind of abuse the evil Stepmother puts on Snow White? Snow White is royalty, yet she is forced to dress in rags and clean the castle. It is made clear that Snow White's father is unfit to take care of his daughter and protect her from her evil stepmother. It may even seem he does not care at all. This family situation instils the longing for her own love, her own man with whom she can start a family and escape from her evil stepmother.

The notion of the traditional family being the ideal is further underlined once Snow White enters the cottage of the dwarfs later on in the film. Whereas in Grimm's fairy tale the cottage is sparkling clean and well kept[20], Walt Disney thought it necessary to change the setting and show us a dirty, unkempt and untidy house. Due to the smaller size of the interior within the cottage, Snow White jumps to the conclusion that it must be seven children living here. However, the untidy state of the cottage prompts Snow White to say: *"You think their mother would... Huh... Maybe they have no mother. [...] I know we'll clean the house to surprise them".* So apparently, a house or a family without a mother will inevitably lead to chaos. And once a woman enters a house or a family, it is her responsibility to establish order and her duty to make the place clean, warm and inhabitable again. This stereotypical depiction is further enforced later on in the movie by two devices.

One of them is the characterization of the dwarfs. They only agree to let Snow White stay, once she offers to keep house and cook for them. Also, their behaviour reminds us more of the antics of children than grown men. At the dinner table they are rowdy and fight over the food and it takes Snow White to calm them down and tell them how to

---

[20] compare http://classiclit.about.com/library/bl-etexts/grimm/bl-grimm-snowwhite.htm [retrieved 28.11.2012, 15:20]

behave and teach them manners. Then, in a very motherly fashion, she reprimands them for not washing their hands before dinner and sends them outside to get clean. Apparently, before Snow White came along, the dwarfs did not understand the concept of personal hygiene. Snow White very obviously acts as a mother figure and the dwarfs are her children.

This assumption is further developed when we get to see the dwarfs dancing and singing and frolicking with Snow White later on in the movie. Whereas the house was cold, dark, and empty in the beginning, now it is filled with music, laughter, and joy – all due to the presence of a woman. It takes a dutiful mother to make a comfortable home.

Cinderella, the second heroine, shows a lot of parallels to Snow White. First her mother dies and although her father is described as being a loving and devoted parent, he himself feels that a little child needs the care of a mother to be happy. Therefore, he marries a woman from a wealthy family, who brings her own two daughters into the marriage. This again supports the notion that the mothers are the care-givers, the soft parents whereas the fathers are the providers of the family.

However, shortly after Cinderella's father also dies and her stepmother and stepsisters turn out to be evil and mean, spending all of the family fortune and forcing Cinderella to do all the housework. So once again our heroine was "abandoned" by her parents and dreams to flee from her home. The only way to do so, is by falling in love and starting her own family. So again, falling in love and marrying a man serve as an escape route.

Cinderella offers another good example for this argument. The King, who desperately wishes for grandchildren and exasperated at his son's (Prince Charming) apparent unwillingness to cooperate and find a suitable wife, exclaims: *"I can't understand it! There must be a least one who'd make a suitable mother! [...] A suitable wife!"*

The heroine in *Sleeping Beauty*, Princess Aurora, is not an orphan. She has two loving parents who are entirely devoted to her. However, not only are they frozen in fear when Maleficent suddenly appears and unable to stop her from uttering the spell, but once Maleficent cursed her with her spell, her parents are powerless to protect her and give her over into the care of the fairy godmothers. Apparently, they themselves are not fit to protect her and she has to be locked away in an isolated cabin, condemning her to a parentless life and unhappiness.

Ariel, Belle and Jasmine as well grow up without mothers and while Ariel is driven away (into the motherly arms of Ursula) by her father's aggression and dominance, Belle and Jasmine are forced to deal with their fathers' antics and clumsiness. Belle has to care for her father Maurice in a motherly fashion, instead of him taking care of her. She encourages him to keep working on his inventions and continuously rescues him when he makes mistakes. In the end it is Maurice's apparent incapability of caring for himself, which leads to Belle exchanging her life for her father's in a bargain with the Beast. *"Indeed, he seems almost helpless without her. In addition, Maurice's appearance, which is similar to that of one of Disney's seven dwarfs, encourages the audience to view him as a child who needs a caretaker. By putting Belle in the role of that caretaker, the Disney Beauty and Beast reinforces the Angel-in-the-House stereotype of woman as responsible for making sure that domestic life goes smoothly."* (Manley, 2003, p. 81)

Mulan even brings shame and dishonour onto her whole family, because she doesn't know how to pour tea or knows the basic rules for a good wife. So her worth as a person and her happiness are directly linked to her potential of finding a good man and be a good mother. As long as she is no marriage material, she will not be happy.

This apparent link between romance, family and happiness in Disney movies is very troubling. Firstly, it may awaken very unrealistic expectations about love and marriage in young children. Also, it directly links happiness to family and children which may entice young girls to believe that fulfilling their traditional roles will be the only way to have a happy and content life. However, nowadays very often it is these gender stereotypes which tie young women down and keep them from fulfilling their potential. Of course, marrying and being a housewife can lead to a very fulfilled and satisfied life, but it also creates a precarious dependence for women on men. Not all marriages are as happy and carefree as depicted in the Disney movies and a financially and emotionally dependent woman will not be able to easily leave her husband. To conclude my argument, I would like to point to Brenda Ayres (2003, p. 33) who wrote: *"[...] Perhaps such gender expectations – that a girl is supposed to grow up to become a wife and a mother – are the poisonous apples. [...] Overtly the emphasis of Disney's message is different. Performing one's traditional gender role within the family is the only way to live happily ever after. Covertly, the poisoned apple [...] is, as Madonna Kolbenschlag puts it, "psychic bondage to men" (42) [...]".*

6.2.3. Demeanour and gender ideologies

When it comes to proper behaviour for women and men according to Disney, it becomes painfully clear that little to no progress has been made. Women should be soft-spoken, obedient, and diligently fulfil their duties and responsibilities. Men are bold, adventurous and most of all, free. I have chosen three recurring themes, which can be found throughout the Princesses' movies, to underline this assumption.

6.2.3.1. Women are obedient and dutiful / Men are strong and heroic

To find evidence for this claim, one does not even have to watch the whole movie, but simply pay attention to how the main characters are introduced.

When Snow White, Cinderella and Aurora, the first three Disney Princesses, get introduced to the audience, all three of them can be seen cleaning and doing housework. Snow White is washing and scrubbing the steps to the palace, as soon as Cinderella is dressed, she starts the chores for the day, and grown-up Aurora is first seen dusting and airing out the house. Their respective princes, on the other hand, are free to roam the land on the backs of their horses, apparently free from any duties or responsibilities. What is even more surprising is that although they are princes, guards or an armada do not surround them, no, they are alone and obviously very capable of taking care of themselves.

One may argue that these princesses are products of the respective time periods during which these films were released, however, newer Disney Princesses show the same pattern again.

The last two heroines – Tiana and Rapunzel – get introduced in much the same way. While Tiana may not do housework, she works two jobs and can always be seen serving customers or cleaning tables. Rapunzel, the latest addition to the Disney Princesses, seems like an uncanny reincarnation of Aurora. Locked away in a tower, Rapunzel's first activities as a grown-up include cooking, sweeping, baking, sawing, making pottery, and the likes.

Again, their respective counterparts – Prince Naveen and Flynn Rider - enjoy all the freedoms Disney heroes normally do. Prince Naveen – although a no-good at work and living off his parent's money – is first seen roaming the streets, charming the ladies, and playing funky jazz with a street band.

When introducing Flynn Rider, Disney does it in the same fashion as they did with Aladdin. Although both are orphans, they do not suffer the same fate as Cinderella or Snow White. This means, they are not under the rule of an evil stepmother or locked away somewhere. Rather, they can be seen high above the roofs of the city, stealing for the good cause and in general just being very careless and carefree.

Our next heroines are not introduced fulfilling their appointed tasks and chores, but rather by defiantly *refusing* to fulfil them. While at first glance this may sound rather promising, at second glance we can see that nothing really has changed.

The characters Ariel and Pocahontas are presented by not being where they are supposed to be. Ariel is supposed to make her musical debut at a concert, but does not show up. When we finally get to see her in person, she can be seen collecting trivia from the human world, which she finds in a shipwreck. However, judging by the angered reaction of her father Triton when he finds her missing and her own shocked exclamation *("Music! The concert! Oh my gosh! My father's gonna kill me!")* when she remembers, the audience can quickly gather that this thoughtless and reckless behaviour should not be approved of. This assumption is further emphasised, when Sebastian – the conductor – blames Ariel for making him the laughing stock. Her defiance cost him his success.

Pocahontas should be in the village helping with collecting the harvest and welcoming the warriors home. Instead she roams the landscape exploring the nature. This dissatisfies her father, who wants her to get married and settle down.

Their counterparts, Prince Eric and John Smith, get presented in the same manner as their predecessors – free to explore the world and accomplish great things. They both sail on a boat, no ties holding them down, free to go wherever they want to go. They even perform similar heroic feats, Eric saving his dog Max from sure death on the burning ship, while John Smith saves a ship's boy from drowning in a storm, impressing us with their bravery and their compassion for others. There is no one to reprimand them or telling them to settle down and get married.

And although the matchmaker does not consider Mulan marriage material for her lack of domicile skills, we still get to see her fulfilling house chores first thing in the morning after waking up.

This pattern of women being obedient and fulfilling their environment's expectations, while the men are free to break the rules and fulfil their own dreams is a recurrent theme throughout all the movies.

We see Aurora ready to give up on love to marry the prince she was promised to as a child (although she only just has been told she actually is a princess), while Prince Philipp tells his father that he simply cannot marry the princess he was promised to, because he wants to marry the woman he loves. We see Cinderella fulfilling all the chores and housework her stepmother and stepsisters appoint her so she might be able to go to the ball, while Prince Charming refuses to comply with his father's request to finally get married and produce an heir to the throne. We see Ariel hurrying back to her father to apologize for missing the concert, while Prince Eric does not show an ounce of regret over rejecting the princess he was supposed to marry.

One could argue that – especially in the newer movies – the princesses do act out and rebel against what is expected of them. However, in most cases this act of rebelliousness is immediately followed by negative consequences and therefore punished.

Belle, the heroine from *Beauty and the Beast* seems to be a very feminist and progressive Disney heroine, seeing how she prefers reading over cooking or other work chores. However, in response to her *"odd"* behaviour, she is a village outcast, again emphasising that this behaviour is not appropriate for a woman. Gaston even articulates that thought, telling Belle that *"it's not right for women to read"* and informing his sidekick that *"soon she starts getting ideas and thinking"*.

The same argument can be heard in *Mulan* when – after speaking out in public – her father is told that he *"would do well to tell [his] daughter to silence her tongue in a man's presence"*. Her father's response: *"Mulan, you dishonour me"*.

After Mulan is found out as a woman, her (nearly naked) form is thrown to the ground in a public display of (physical) male dominance, while she is being called *"a treacherous snake"* that dishonours the whole Chinese army. All her feats as a "male soldier" weigh nothing against the fact that a woman transgressed her assigned (social) boundaries and ventured (and succeeded) in male territory.

Triton violently destroys Ariel's whole collection of human trivia after he finds out she defied him and went to the surface again to see the humans.

One could even go as far as arguing that Tiana gets punished for trying to "usurp" her designated role. She is supposed to be a black, working class girl, but at the costume ball she dresses up as a princess. Prince Naveen (already turned into a frog), who believes her to be a real princess, talks her into kissing him which results in Tiana being transformed into a frog as well. Put differently, Tiana being turned into a frog is her punishment for her pretence to be someone of higher status than her own and therefore deceiving the prince.

In her thesis, Christine Yzaguirre (2006, p. 46-47) argues that there is *"a clear difference between Disney's older heroines and newer heroines in terms of their personality traits"*. While the older princesses like Snow White, Aurora and Cinderella tend to obey and accept the social norms and show submissive behaviour patterns, *"[...] newer heroines rebel against what is expected of them [...]"*. Yzaguirre even describes some new princesses as being dominant, seeing as they *"[...] have evolved into active go-getters within their plots"*.

As stated before, at first look this impression might seem true. However, as indicated above, in every case this act of rebellion is being received negatively by the environment, therefore telling us that it is *wrong*. In addition, the initially rebellious attitude is almost always being substituted by a concluding settling into traditional roles. In most cases, the act of rebellion serves the heroines to emancipate themselves from their parents or their community to eventually settle into their own (romantic) relationship. Kellie Bean (2003, p. 53) argues that " *[w]hen moving a female character into marriage, Disney first establishes her unfitness for that revered (in the land of Disney) institution, then transforms her into the standard, deserving Disney wife – that is, a voluptuously modest, submissive partner to a rescuing, dominant prince"*.

Richard Finkelstein (2003, p. 137) points to the same thing, stating that *"Ariel's rebelliousness gives way to accommodation with a different patriarchal system: In the end, she integrates herself within a society where her husband's role supplants her father's".*[21]

Brenda Ayres (2003, p. 43) concludes that *"Snow White overtly attempts to Disneyfy its viewers into gender conformity through indictments against rebellious women".*

This means, the princesses are rewarded for their (finally) proper behaviour; if they are obedient and submissive they find love, get married, and start their own families. At the same time, Disney apparently does not appreciate independent women who make their own choices and have their own resources.

The evil stepmothers of Snow White, Cinderella and Rapunzel or Ursula are prime examples of this philosophy. They are (economically and emotionally) independent (from men) and free to make their own choices, therefore – in Disney terms – they have to be bad. Ayres (2003, p. 39) argues that Snow White's stepmother does not represent a proper role model *"because she seems to be independent, self-assertive, resourceful, and free of male domination and influence".*

To emphasise this, strong women in Disney movies are often represented as witches (while "good" women using magic are fairies). *"When the Queen resorts to witchcraft, the audience is supposed to understand her behaviour and her practice as evil. Actually, the film promotes any source of female empowerment as evil."* Ayres (2003, p. 43)

---

[21] There are further scenes in the film, which can be interpreted as Triton and Eric – representing two different patriarchal spheres – "fighting" over Ariel. In a first "battle" Triton symbolically wins by destroying Eric's bust and "beheading" him. However, in the end Eric wins the "war" by defeating Ursula (who defeated Triton). Eric "obtains" Ariel as a prize, who got legs by Triton and left home to marry him.

Finkelstein (2003, p. 145, Note 10) notes as well that *"one sees Disney suggesting that when "female" qualities triumph, they transmute themselves into a tyrannous version of positive patriarchy"*.

Another example for this (although on a smaller scale) is the depiction of the match-maker in Mulan. She is an (apparently) single woman, deciding which girl "can be married" and therefore will bring honour to her family, which puts her in an extremely powerful position. This power and influence is greatly undermined by her portrayal as an ugly, hysteric, and unlikeable woman. At one point, she inadvertently draws herself a moustache with paint on her face, de-feminizing her even more and illustrating the fact that her position is too powerful to be held by a (feminine) woman.

It is easy to see why these princesses do not represent good role models to children, especially young girls. They promote a lifestyle, where young girls are not free to make their own choices and seek self-fulfilment. Rather, their happiness depends on the wishes and expectations of their (male dominated) environment and any act of emancipation yields negative consequences and retribution. Women in powerful positions are painted as unlikeable and undesirable, further reinforcing traditional gender ideologies.

6.2.3.2. Women as civilizing force

The film *Beauty and the Beast* breaks ranks in that the movie highlights a different role model for women than which can be seen in the other movies. Belle, the heroine, acts primarily as a civilizing force for the men around her.

Her own father Maurice is a chaotic klutz and completely overwhelmed with the responsibilities of being a single father. Actually, he can barely take care of himself. Therefore, Belle does not behave like a daughter towards Maurice, but rather like she herself is the parent. She takes care of him, takes care of the housework and in the end it is her who frees Maurice from the Beast. *"Belle's role is to provide a civilizing force for her father by taking care of him. She provides the domestic comfort he needs to continue his work."* (Manley, 2003, p. 81)

Belle would also have been a civilizing force for Gaston, who is presented as *"the epitome of an uncivilized person, believing in the use of force rather than rational discus-*

sion, having no interest in the arts, and lacking respect for those he believes to be physically weaker than he (such as Belle and Maurice)" (Manley, 2003, p. 82). Although Gaston has no understanding of and for Belle's interest in books and even mocks her for her independent lifestyle, he still wants Belle to marry him. He envisions a traditional wife, who cooks and cleans for him and bears him many children. This depiction of their possible family life together serves to show her "taming" influence on a brute like Gaston.

Lastly, Belle is most definitely a civilizing force for the Beast. When we first get to see the Beast, he is mean, aggressive, and violent. He growls, threatens, screams, and rages around. When in rage he throws items and is not hesitant to use physical force to get his will. *"The Disney Studios [...] created a Beast who, in both the film and the book, behaves like a spoiled child; his bestiality is that of a 'little monster' [...]."* (Manley, 2003, p. 84)

In a way, this behaviour makes sense, seeing the timeframe Disney presents in the movie. In the movie the Beast is close to his 21st birthday, as apparent by the rose[22]. In the song *Human again* Lumiere sings that they have been under the spell for 10 years. This means that the Beast must have been put under the spell at the age of 11[23] and spent his whole puberty in the form of the Beast and without human contact. Therefore, his childlike attitude is actually quite reasonable within the setting of the movie, yet *"[b]ecause of the Disney characterization of the Beast as a spoiled child, Belle's relationship to him is much more that of [a] civilizing force [...]"*. (Manley, 2003, p. 84)

This need to *"civilize and nurture him"* (Manley, 2003, p. 84) can be seen throughout the whole movie. Although this time the Disney heroine does not do the chores herself, Belle gives the impulse for the enchanted servants to clean up the whole castle, therefore once again demonstrating the need for a women to have a clean house. She teaches the Beast manners, to eat properly, to read, to dance, to be kind to the servants and other

---

[22] On this date, the rose loses its last petal according to the curse.

[23] This (surprisingly) young age prompts two questions: Firstly, why is the prince in the beginning of the movie already presented as an adult? And secondly, it also leads us to the question of the whereabouts of his family and – as they are never even mentioned – their apparent absence once again implies the underlying message that non-traditional family settings (the prince may not have had parents, but he had hundreds of servants who cared for him) are not ideal and therefore doomed to fail.

beings, and when injured she bandages his arm and stays with him. She softens his attitude, turning him into a kind and gentle being, effectively *"encouraging him to become
an adult who might be a reasonable suitor"*. (Manley, 2003, p. 85)

Manley (2003, p. 84) further argues that *"though a women in Belle's situation might see
that situation as one where she can wield power, a more adult response is annoyance;
the mothering, civilizing role does not provide an adult-to-adult relationship"*. Ayres
further underlines this by stating that although *"Belle [...] [is a] female who [is] obviously superior in character to [her] male counterpart, [...] [she is] to invest all of [her]
resources toward making [her man] successful"*. (Ayres, 2003, p. 48)

Women as civilizing force can also be seen in other movies, although not as prominently as in *Beauty and the Beast*. One of the seven dwarfs in *Snow White* is called
'Grumpy'. Like his name suggests, he is a rather unpleasant fellow, who is very suspi-
cious of Snow White as he despises women in general. While all the other dwarfs immediately fall in love with Snow White, Grumpy repeatedly warns them to not fall prey
to her charm. In the end however, all of Snow Whites cleaning and cooking and especially her public display of affection (kissing the dwarfs on the head) pays off, as
Grumpy's demeanour gradually softens and in the end he is the first to run to her rescue.

Also in *Pocahontas* we can see this theme, although in a much broader fashion. When
the swelling conflict between the Native Americans and the Settlers climaxes, the audience gets to see both sides preparing for war. The male Native Americans paint their
faces, sharpen their weapons and pray to their gods, while the Settlers as well arm themselves heavily. The whole scene is accompanied by a song called *Savages* where both
sides paint the other as monsters respectively. We see them marching off to war, both
opposing parties not ready to budge. Finally, when the Chief of the Native Americans
(Pocahontas' father) prepares to execute John Smith, it is Pocahontas who throws herself over John Smith protectively, telling her father that he will have to kill them both. It
is that act of bravery from Pocahontas, which convinces her father to lower his weapon
and tell his people to step back. In response the Settlers do the same. Pocahontas man-
aged to civilize not only one, but two armies of men and in effect prevented a war.

I chose to discuss this particular theme because I think it has the potential of transporting a very dangerous message to young girls. Young girls (and also boys) should be taught that violence is never acceptable. Yet, these movies *"[send] a strong message reinforcing the stereotypical belief that a beautiful women is a civilizing force capable of taming the beast in a man"* (Manley, 2003, p. 87), *"it may also cause women to have an unrealistic belief in their ability to reform a man who treats them badly"* (Maio, 1992, p. 45, as cited in Manley, 2003, p. 88).

6.2.3.3. Women as instruments

Another gender ideology I would like to highlight, is the use of women as means to an end. To illustrate my point I have chosen Ariel, Jasmine, and Mulan as examples, as those three very clearly show how women are used as instruments by their environment.

I want to start with Ariel the mermaid. Ariel is an instrument to various other characters under the sea. First of all, she is an instrument to her father. Triton, king of the mer-world, is presented as a very masculine character. In a splendorous event he wants to present his youngest and fairest daughter. The daughters are the *"pride of Triton"*, who *"named them well"*. The sole purpose of showcasing the daughters is to strengthen Triton's image as a potent man and father. Ariel not showing up to the concert exposes him to ridicule and – in a way – takes away from his masculinity.

Not showing up to the concert also angers Sebastian, the conductor. Although he had six other well-singing girls, all depended on Ariel alone. Her absence made him the laughing stock. She – or more especially her unique voice – was his instrument to reach glory and acclaim as a conductor. He was not furious with her for not showing up, but rather because her defiance cost him his success and exposed him to ridicule as well. As Finkelstein (2003, p. 142) points out, *"[a]ll want to manage Ariel's voice in much the same way that they want to control her use of her body [...]"*.

However, Ariel being used as an instrument for the sole purpose of reaching a different goal is mostly highlighted by Ursula. Ursula actually has no interest in hurting Ariel personally, but wants to use her to get revenge on Triton, as the *"pretty little daughter"* is *"the key to Triton's undoing"*. Therefore, even to Ursula, Ariel herself has no worth as a person, but rather her worth is determined by how much she can hurt Triton. This is made clear as Ursula tells her two eel servants that *"Triton's daughter will be mine, and I'll make him writhe. I'll see him wriggle like a worm on a hook."*

Jasmine, the Disney Princess from the movie *Aladdin*, is another example for this particular gender ideology.

For her father, it is necessary that she marries so he can uphold the law. Although he understands that his daughter wants love in a marriage, in order for his reign to remain stable, Jasmine needs to marry one of her suitors.

For Jafar, the villain, Jasmine becomes an instrument to reach his goal of becoming the Sultan. When his first plan of finding the magical lamp with the Genie failed, Jasmine's defiance to marry one of her suitors plays into his cards. Using a magical trick he convinces the Sultan that there is a law, stating that the Royal Vizier of Agrabah (Jafar's position in court) should marry the princess if she cannot or will not decide on her own. Once married, Jafar schemes to get rid of the Sultan and succeed him on the throne. This means that Jasmine's sole purpose to Jafar is to enable him to become Sultan.

To Aladdin, Jasmine presents the means to climb up the social ladder. By wishing to be transformed into a prince by the Genie and courting Jasmine, Aladdin hopes to make Jasmine fall in love with him. Although Aladdin initially wishes to be prince to be an eligible suitor for Jasmine and win her over, he is quickly drawn into the lavish lifestyle. Soon he can be seen negotiating an arranged marriage with the Sultan and Jafar, indicating that Aladdin is prepared to disregard Jasmine's (possibly negative) feelings on this matter, as the outlook of a better life off the streets became more appealing than winning Jasmine's love.

In *Mulan* as well, there are undertones of this theme, as *"[u]ltimately, her demonstrated feats of bravery, fighting skill, and intelligence serve to bring honour to her father and prove her worthy of the captain's love"*. (Ayres, 2003, p. 48)

6.2.4. Physical Appearance & Sexual Desire

After reviewing and analyzing the movies, it is clear that the animation and visualisation of the princesses and their respective princes has changed little in the past 75 years.

The princesses are all of small stature (apart from Pocahontas) and thin. They all have very small waists, which emphasises their breasts and their hips (to different degrees), giving them a voluptuous and sandglass-like figure. Although in most movies the characters are still adolescents or have barely passed puberty, this animation of their bodies gives them a much more sexualised and mature appearance.

Their faces are round and youthful, with big round or almond-shaped eyes, small noses, small mouths and beautiful skin. They exclusively have long hair and wear dresses or skirts (apart from Mulan, who cuts her long hair off in the beginning for her disguise as a man). The princesses do not wear make-up (apart from Jasmine) to emphasise their naturalness and youth.

The princes are all of a tall stature (apart from Aladdin), sporting muscular and athletic frames. Most of them have strong legs, broad shoulders, and a wide chest giving them a very masculine and trained look. Their hair-length ranges between short to medium-length. The earlier princes have slightly rounder faces, while newer princes have slightly more angles and edges (especially John Smith). What is curious though is that none of the princes has a beard or has any other kind of bodily hair. This allows them to remain youthful and juvenile despite their very masculine physical appearance.

When compared to other female and male characters, it becomes clear that above listed characteristics are signifiers for "good". Put differently, naturally beautiful girls and masculine boys are to be understood as having good characters, while girls and boys with different visual looks are to be met with suspicion. Disney uses several visual devices to set the princesses and princes apart from other female characters.

The most illustrating example for the "beautiful-is-good" stereotype are Cinderella's sisters. Compared to Cinderella, they are not fair at all. They have big noses and two lines on their face, which give them a much older and crumpled look. This visual depiction comes hand in hand with them being lazy, arrogant, and haughty.

Another means to stereotype women is an off-size body. Although Maleficent and the evil stepmothers in the early Disney Princess movies are all thin, they are overly so. Due to their tallness, they do not seem well proportioned but rather lanky. Ursula the sea-witch is very round and voluptuous. Also, they all wear make-up. The audience is to understand this unnaturalness as something bad, which is not to be desired.

Disney also denies powerful women the female signifier of long, lose hair[24]. The hair of Snow White's stepmother and Maleficent is covered by clothing. The hair of Cinderella's stepmother is tied up in a bun. Ursula has short hair. The matchmaker in Mulan has her hair tied back. Gothel (*Rapunzel*) is actually the first female villain to sport long, lose hair. This is important as it de-feminizes the women. The lack of loose hair combined with their increased tallness and physical presence implies male characteristics. This visualisation is trying to indicate to the viewer that women in powerful positions are more male than female and therefore (sexually) not desirable.

On the other hand, males with lose, long hair have a negative connotation too. A very illustrative example for this is the movie *Mulan*, where all the Chinese soldiers have their hair tied back, while the Huns wear their long hair open. Also Radcliffe, the villain in the movie Pocahontas, has long hair, which he wears in a tail. Jafar wears a turban with an attached veil, which gives off the impression of long hair. Here, these visual devices serve to emasculate the characters.

What is interesting to see, is that this visual emasculation of male characters in Disney movies often serves as a device to express a hierarchal order in a patriarchal system. Very often, the prince is the only "real" man and therefore ranks first in the hierarchy. Naturally, this legitimizes him as the obvious suitor for the princess. If this visual device is not used, then the conflicts between two apparent "alpha males" are solved with violence.[25]

In Snow White, the dwarfs are more reminiscent of children than of men, due to their animation and visualisation. Therefore, they pose no threat to the prince in terms of ro-

---

[24] Sheng-mei Ma (2003, p. 156) discusses the importance of hair in her essay on Disney's Mulan: *"The hair fetish in Mulan is elevated from a symbol of gorgeous looks to one of gender, the pivotal motif in this story of cross dressing. [...] The only moments when her hair is loosened are when her identity is at risk of being revealed".*

[25] In *The Little Mermaid* and *Pocahontas*, where this conflict of two males is not resolved artistically, it is done through violence. Eric's triumph over Ursula is a triumph over Triton as well, who was defeated by Ursula. John Smith and Kocoum fight and as a result Kocoum gets killed (not by John Smith though).

mance, even though Snow White is living with them. In Cinderella, the only other visible men apart from the prince are his father and his father's advisor. While the father is rather round and plump and behaves extremely childish, the advisor is presented as tall, lanky and fearful. This pattern can be seen in *Sleeping Beauty* as well, where the father's again behave like children, posing no threat to the prince. In *Aladdin* again, the Sultan is very childlike and immature, whereas Jafar has decisively female facial features, especially his eyes.

Exaggeration is another visual device Disney likes to employ. Overly sexualised girls or girls who are very invested in their looks are often portrayed as bimbo-like or stupid. Examples of this are the three sisters in *Beauty and the Beast*, Ariel's sisters or Charlotte, the best friend of Tiana in *The Princess and the Frog*. On the other hand, it can also mean bad or evil, as illustrated with Ursula, the sea-witch in *The Little Mermaid*. She is first seen putting on make-up and painting her lips red. Her body is inviting the audience to indulge in every possible way and she moves smoothly and oozes sexual power.

Figure 11: Ursula, Source: http://disney.wikia.com/ wiki/File:12357.gif

Gaston, in a way, can be seen as Ursula's male counterpart in respect to exaggerated gender related features. He is very muscular, almost too muscular. As the only Disney man he sports chest hair. His face is very angled and he has a very prominent chin. However, he as well is very vain and concerned with his looks. Manley (2003, p. 82) argues that Gaston's look combined with his character serve to mark him as the true beast, an *"epitome of an uncivilized person"*.

One of the implications of this focal point on looks and beauty in Disney movies is that often, women become objects of desire for men. They are not wanted for their personal traits or accomplishments, but rather for their unique physique and beauty. *"They are*

Figure 12: Gaston
Source: http://disney.wikia.com/wiki/File:Gaston.jpg

male-defined fantasies of female biological perfection." (Bean, 2003, p. 55)

A moment which echoes this sentiment very clearly, is the scene in *The Little Mermaid*, when Ursula asks for Ariel's voice in exchange for human legs. Ariel is confused and starts to ask *"But without my voice, how can I – "* and gets cut off by Ursula with the following advice:

You'll have your looks, your pretty face.
And don't underestimate the importance of body language, ha!

The men up there don't like a lot of blabber / They think a girl who gossips is a bore!
Yet on land it's much preferred for ladies not to say a word / And after all dear, what is idle babble for?
Come on, they're not all that impressed with conversation / True gentlemen avoid it when they can
But they dote and swoon and fawn / On a lady who's withdrawn
It's she who holds her tongue who gets a man

The line *"And don't underestimate the importance of body language, ha!"* is accompanied by Ursula jiggling her massive hips and breasts and throwing her head back. The message is clear: hold your tongue, use your body and you'll get a man.

Another example is Belle, whose beauty makes her the best choice to marry according to Gaston. At one point he claims *"I've got my sights set upon this one"*, emphasising his role as the hunter and Belle's role as the prey. *"Belle's beauty is an object he wishes to possess [...]."* (Manley, 2003, p. 82)

As can be seen above, gender-roles for women and men respectively in Disney movies have not changed much over the past decades. Of course the themes discussed do not cover the entirety of gender issues raised in Disney Princess movies, however, they give a good overlook over the most dominant and persistent stereotypes (re-)produced.

6.3. Racial & Ethnic Stereotypes

While the above presented analysis focused solely on gender stereotypes, this sub-chapter will deal with racial and ethnic stereotypes in Disney Princess movies. One could argue that creating movies, whose setting and main characters introduce new and foreign cultures to our children is something to be appreciated. However, bearing in mind that these stories are not only retold, but also reinterpreted by a US-based company run primarily by white men[26], the presented depictions of different ethnic groups warrant a closer and critical look.

When discussing ethnic stereotypes in the Disney Princess movies, we will take a closer look at *Aladdin*, *Pocahontas*, *Mulan* and *The Princess and the Frog*. However, in a way also the other movies can be viewed as reproducing ethnic stereotypes by the *lack* of diversity and stipulating a world "dominated by white". The following chapter will show how ethnic groups (other than "white") are represented in the Disney Princess movies and how these portrayals transport racial stereotypes to children.

6.3.1. Varied racial depiction and its implication

What can be noticed right away is the varied depiction of characters of the same race. While at first thought this does not seem far-fetched, since diversity also exists within one ethnic group, in this particular case it does present a troubling picture.

A good example for this is the movie *Aladdin*. In this movie, all the protagonists are considerable lighter skinned and more westernized as the antagonists. All the Arab men in the movie wear a black beard or moustache apart from Aladdin, who has no beard, and the Sultan, having a white beard. The faces of the likeable characters (Jasmine, Aladdin, Sultan) are round and juvenile with big eyes, while the palace guards or Jafar have sharp angles, big noses and slit eyes.

Figure 13: Aladdin and Jafar, Source: http://i19.photobucket.com/albums/b1 91/AladdinsGenie/For%20Friends/ala ddin005295.png

---

[26]   compare   http://thewaltdisneycompany.com/about-disney/leadership/management   [retrieved 26.01.2013, 18:30]

The same can be seen in the movie *Mulan*, where the depiction of the Chinese people and the Huns – the protagonists and the antagonists respectively – is starkly different. Whereas the Chinese people do have ethnical features, like slightly darker skin, black hair, and almond-shaped eyes, their faces and depictions are still westernized, especially when compared to the Huns. Their skin is more wheat-coloured than dark, marking a closer resemblance to white. Their faces are round and friendly. Again, Shang is one of the few men without a beard, giving him a smooth and youthful look.

The Huns on the other hand are depicted as rampaging savages, which are downright animalistic. They have grey skin, loose black hair, and very tall frames. Their sharp-angled faces come with yellow, hawk-like eyes, and teeth, which seem more like fangs. Their fingernails resemble claws and when they speak, it is more like a growl.

Figure 14: Shan Yu, Source: http://images4.wikia.nocookie.net/_cb20120413171941/villains/images/5/50/Shanyu_ref_%281%2911.jpg

This trend can be seen continued in *The Princess and the Frog*, which features the first African-American princess. Tiana does have darker skin and a slightly broader nose, however, her facial features still include big round eyes and a small mouth and her frame is – like the others – petite with a very small waist. In *The Princess and the Frog* though, it is another character, which causes some racial-related issues.

Obviously, Disney was prepared to give their audience the first African-American princess, yet, the princess did not get her black-skinned prince; rather Prince Naveen is much lighter than Tiana. Admittedly, the depiction of an interracial couple can be seen as positive and progressive, however in this case, it does raise some questions.

The focal point of criticism lies on the racial ambiguousness of Prince Naveen. Although the movie is set in New Orleans (therefore a real city), Prince Naveen comes from an invented country which does not exist. His body is tall and strong, resembling white men, while his face and his complexion bears resemblance to people of Latin descent. He speaks with a Brazilian accent and when we get to see his parents in the end, they look like they come from India.

It seems that Disney did not dare to present the audience with two explicitly black main characters, in fear of scaring them off. (It is harder to "lighten" up supposedly black characters.) However, apparently they also did not dare to put her with a man from a distinctively recognizable different race, in order to avoid questioning why Tiana is the first princess to not get a prince of her own ethnicity[27]. This way, they seemingly hoped to get a win-win situation in that people of African-American descent finally (it only took 75 years) get their black princess and to retain their "white" audience by giving them a prince they could (at least) relate to.

Figure 15: Tiana and Prince Naveen, Source: http://images2.fanpop.com/image/photos/1090 0000/tiana-and-naveen-after-wedding-the-princess-and-the-frog-10977173-1280-800.jpg

And again, the antagonist – Dr. Facilier – is portrayed starkly different than the other characters. His skin is a kind of mocha, he is tall and lanky, with a big, prominent chin and a moustache. His face consists of sharp angles and he sports a gap between his two front teeth. While his visual depiction may not assign him to one distinctive ethnicity, the fact that he is a "witch doctor" who practices voodoo implies that he is of Haitian descent.

Lee Artz (2004, p. 5) points to the fact that in general, *"[g]ood characters (e. g., [...], the Sultan, Ariel, Pocahontas) exhibit juvenile traits such as big eyes and round cheeks (Lawrence, 1986, p. 67) and are drawn in curves, smooth, round, soft, bright and with European features; villains (e.g., [...] , Jafar, the Hun, Ratcliffe, Ursula) are drawn with sharp angles, oversized, and often darkly".*

---

[27] Although Pocahontas and John Smith were of different ethnicities, they did not end up as a couple.

It becomes clear that Disney westernizes its main ethnic characters to closer resemble white characters. More prominent or even exaggerated depictions of ethnic features and signifiers are used to identify the antagonists and characters with hurtful intentions.

This is revelant, as Dotsch (2001) establishes that *"[b]ecause faces are an important source of information to establish category membership, group members' typical facial appearance is likely to be included in the visual stereotype. A newly formed visual stereotype might simply entail aggregating all previously encountered group members' facial configurations. On the other hand, faces are not just pure feature configurations, but take on social meaning as people infer traits from face".* (Todorov et al. 2008, Zebrowitz & Montepare 2008, as cited in Dotsch, 2001, p. 4)

This means, by westernizing and in a way "bleaching" its ethnic main characters, Disney counts on the fact that, due to pre-existing stereotypes and prejudice, the audience will view the ethnic protagonists as more "white" and therefore one of them[28]. This also explains why Aladdin – an Arab boy – is modelled after Tom Cruise rather than a random street boy of Bagdad. (see Staninger, 2003, p. 67)

However, seeing as Disney obviously uses ethnical signifiers (no matter the culture) to point out the bad guys, it also highlights the great danger that lies within these movies. Being constantly bombarded with negatively connoted images of other races, children will be more likely inclined to form negative stereotypes or prejudices in regards to "others" in general.

6.3.2. The Coloured Princesses

I chose to discuss this particular theme, because when it comes to the coloured princesses in the Disney Princess movies, two contrary observations can be made. Either the female main characters are overly sexualised (especially when compared with the white princesses) or they are not shown in traditional female roles (or even as females) throughout most of the movies.

---

[28] This makes sense, seeing how in the financial year 2010, the company derived 74.3% of its revenues from the US and Canada. However, the company has little presence in markets like Asia or Latin America. (They only accounted for 8.5% of the company's total revenue. (Source: SWOT Analysis by datamonitor [www.datamonitor.com])

The first coloured princess was Jasmine in *Aladdin*. Although Jasmine's skin tone is slightly darker and she has long black hair – as is appropriate for a Middle Eastern setting – the rest of her face and body retain many features, which are signifiers for "whiteness". Her eyes are more almond-shaped than round, but other than that she still has a very small nose and mouth. Her frame as well is very petite and like all the princesses before her, she sports a very small waist. As her design does not offer a lot of signifiers of racial difference, which could set her apart from the white princesses before her, Disney chose to illustrate her "orientalism" through her clothing. Jasmine sports wide pants in typically Eastern design, which accentuates her hips. Her top accentuates her breasts, while leaving her stomach and shoulders bare. All of these features put together, result in Jasmine giving off a much more adult and sexual look than her predecessors.

Figure 16: Jasmine, Source: http://disney-clipart.com/Aladdin/jasmine/Princess-Jasmine3.php

Another stark difference to the princesses before her is the use of make-up when designing Jasmine, whereas before, the use of make-up was employed to signify "bad" women (see Maleficent or Ursula) and to emphasise the "naturalness" of the heroines.

This look is further emphasised by her very flirtatious behaviour. Whereas the white princesses before her where very shy and innocent, Jasmine is very self-assured and active. Her whole movement and body language is very open, flirtatious and at times even teasing. After Aladdin saved her in the market place, they go up to his "home" where – after a rather short talk – they lean in to kiss. They only reason they do not is the arrival of the guards. At some points, she can even be heard throwing slightly sexual innuendos at Aladdin and in general she is using her body to her advantage.

Later in the movie, when Jafar is Sultan, we can see Jasmine in red clothes, which are even more revealing and her hair tied up, to show more of her neck, shoulders and cleavage. It is implied that Jafar dressed her up this way for his (sexual) enjoyment (i.a. he calls her "pussycat"). When Aladdin comes to the rescue, we can see Jasmine using her sexual power over Jafar to distract him, even going as far as kissing him.

Film Analysis & Discussion

Figure 17: Dancing girls in *Aladdin*,
Source: still from the movie

But it is not only Jasmine, which gets presented in this way. There are several moments throughout the movie, where we can see scantily clad women, very often belly-dancing.

When Aladdin first meets the Genie, he shows Aladdin the possibilities of what he can do for him. Among other things, he conjures three dancing women, who are barely wearing more than underwear, sporting wide hips, big breasts and an impossible-to-reach wasp waist.

Also, when Aladdin – already a prince – parades into the town, again nearly naked women with wide hips, big breasts and small waists can be seen dancing and fawning over Aladdin. Even the Genie, when imitating a woman, is sporting make-up, big breasts and a bare belly.

What makes this even more troubling is the depiction of "normal" women in town. When showing scenes where the common crowd can be seen, women wear clothes which cover their whole body. They wear head scarves and non-see-through veils over their faces. Their eyes are much smaller and their bodies are plumper.

Figure 18: "Normal" women in *Aladdin*, Source: still from the movie

Pocahontas differs from her predecessors in a similar fashion. Her skin tone is slightly darker, owing to her Native American heritage. However, compared to most of her tribe she is still slightly lighter-skinned than the rest. Her facial features reveal big eyes, a small nose and lush lips. Pocahontas is exceptional compared to all the other princesses, as she has a very tall frame, strong legs and an overall athletic body. Also, her bust is much bigger. However, as the rest, she retains the small waist. This, in combination with her bigger bust, gives her a very adult and voluptuous look, especially when compared to princesses like Snow White, Aurora or Belle.

Figure 19: Pocahontas,
Source: http://disney.wikia.com/wiki/Pocahontas_%28character%29

81 | P a g e

LaCroix points out that the design of Pocahontas generated lot of critical response, especially the fact that her *"physique [...] reflected a body structure comparable to that of a Barbie Doll, or supermodel"*. (LaCroix, 2004, p. 220)

Like Jasmine, Pocahontas is also not as naive about men as the other princesses were. In fact, measured in Disney-standard, her relationship with John Smith is actually a very grown-up relationship. There is a lot of physical touch between them, as well as clandestine meetings and stolen kisses.

It is important to consider this starkly different visual and characteristical representation of Jasmine and Pocahontas, as LaCroix (2004) points out that *"[i]n particular, the representation of gender and race and a pattern of increasing orientalization reveal themselves in the characters' physical characteristics"* (p. 217) and *"[i]n tracing the progression of the physical presentation of female heroines in these Disney films, one can chart a movement toward increasingly physical (and sexual) maturity"* (p. 218). LaCroix (2004, p. 227) further illustrates that in Disney animated film, there is *"a pattern of increasing orientalization of women of colour"*. Sexual stereotypes, particularly with regards to women of colour, are used to *"exoticise female characters"*.

This is made even more prominent when comparing Jasmine and Pocahontas to Rapunzel. Rapunzel is the first white Disney Princess after four coloured princesses and she is a spitting image of Disney's earliest princesses. A round face with big eyes, a small nose, a small mouth, and long blond hair. She sports a petite frame and although her waist as well is very small, her breasts are not as prominently featured, therefore giving her body a more adolescent appearance. And although she is a very active and headstrong character, her demeanour regarding men and male attention is again very shy and naive and not as sexually charged.

Figure 20: Rapunzel, Source: http://disney.wikia.com/ wiki/Rapunzel

Mulan and Tiana, the other two coloured heroines, differ from Jasmine and Pocahontas, as they are not presented as overly sexualised characters. Although this may sound promising at first, this break in visualisation is not owed to a change of heart of the Disney animators, but rather to storylines which puts them in non-female (or non-human) roles throughout most of the movies.

Mulan is dressed as a man most time of the movie. However, when appearing on-screen as a girl, certain parallels to the other princesses can be made. Again, she is has a round face with a small nose and small lips. Her eyes are more almond-shaped, but that is due to her Chinese heritage. She has light skin and a very petite frame. In the beginning of the movie she has long black hair, which she cuts off so she can pose as a man.

Mulan's depiction regarding her attitude towards men is not as overtly sexually charged as is Pocahontas' or Jasmine's, but she does not seem to be too naive either. When Shang takes off his shirt to train, we can see her stare appreciatively. In another scene, Mulan steals off to take bath and gets interrupted by three fellow sol-

Figure 21: Mulan as soldier
Source:
http://disney.wikia.com/
wiki/File:Mulanaspingart.png

diers. As the men are unaware that Mulan is actually a woman, they are rather unreserved concerning their bodies and at some point Mulan gets to see one of them naked. Although her reaction is to look away slightly flustered and cover her eyes, she does not react overly fussed about it either. Actually her anxiety in this particular scene stems more from the fear of her secret being discovered, than her being seen naked or seeing someone naked.

Tiana is the first African-American Disney Princess. Accordingly she has dark skin and black hair. Her facial features do differ slightly, in that she has a slightly bigger nose and her eyes are a bit further apart. However, she still has big, round eyes and a small mouth. Also, her body does present the same picture. She is rather small of stature with a very small waist, but at times a seemingly slightly bigger bottom. What is a bit surprising is the structure of her hair, as it seems rather sleek and not as fizzy as often seen with people of African-American origin.

When in human form, Tiana is dressed and comports herself very modestly. However, in the scenes, where an Art Deco graphic style is employed, Tiana is sporting much fancier clothes, which are more revealing and also her comportment is more self-assured.

6.3.3. Language & Accents

In Disney movies, not only visual devices are used to reinforce cultural stereotypes, but also auditory means. By using different accents or ethnically coded language, Disney often uses stereotypes to help create the image of a character. As this particular issue with Disney movies is actually more prominent in movies which feature animal characters (as opposed to humans)[29], I will just give a brief glimpse into the topic.

In the movie *Aladdin*, accents are used to differentiate between protagonists and antagonists. In tandem with the visual depiction (see above), characters which have a lower status or are not as likeable speak with a noticeable accent. Good characters speak accent-free English.

In *Beauty and the Beast* accents are used to appoint ethnicities. The chandelier speaks with a noticeable French accent, as do the dust-sweepers. The clock and the teapot however have British accents. The French chandelier and dust-sweepers obviously enjoy a savoir-vivre lifestyle, which includes indulgence, flirtation, and pleasure. The British clock in contrast is very uptight and stiff, and the British teapot is friendly and tidy. Hence, the culturally coded language in *Beauty and the Beast* serves to activate certain stereotypes the audience may have about these cultures, which allows them to better connect to the exposed behaviour of the enchanted furniture and which makes them more human.

---

[29] Lee Artz (2004) argues that race, gender and class act as recurring indicators of hierarchy. In movies featuring animals, visual signifiers cannot be used to appoint a certain ethnicity to a character, therefore, auditory signifiers have to be used. A good example for this are the hyenas in "The Lion King" as Artz notes that *"[i]n the* Lion King, *Mustafa not only talks, he talks with the diction and accent of British nobility, while the hyenas act and sound like stereotypically black and Latino urban youth"*. (p. 121)

In the movie *The little Mermaid*, the crab Sebastian talks with a Jamaican accent. This has been the focus of some criticism[30] as Sebastian sings a song which is called *Under the Sea*. Some critics have interpreted the lyrics (and also the accompanying visual depiction) as racist, as, among others, Sebastian describes life under the sea as time being spent doing nothing and basically fish just jamming together all day long:

Up on the shore they work all day / Out in the sun they slave away

While we devotin' / Full time to floatin'

Under the sea

What makes these lines so problematic is indeed the fact that they stem from a character with a Jamaican accent. This has the potential of (subconsciously) reinforcing negative stereotypes about people of Jamaican descent.

The same argument is valid for the firefly Ray in *The Princess and the Frog*, who speaks with a Cajun accent. In this case however, it is not so much the content of what the firefly says, which is troubling, but the pairing of visual and auditory depiction of the character.

Ray is a laid-back, at times seemingly confused character, who shows big tooth-holes when he smiles. Although he has a loving and gentle heart, at times he does seem slow on the up-take and in general is presented as a dreamer, who has his head up in the clouds.

The Council for the Development of French in Louisiana had taken an issue with the portrayal of the Cajun character. The CODOFIL is a state agency, which is charged with the protection and promotion of French in Louisiana. Their President Warren Perrin stated, that the portrayal of Ray is *"[...] a continuation of the stereotyping of Cajun*

Figure 22: Firefly Ray from *The Princess and the Frog*, Source: http://disney.wikia.com/ wiki/Ray?file=Princess-And-The-Frog-Ray.jpg

---

[30] compare http://www.cracked.com/article_15833_the-9-most-racist-disney-characters.html [retrieved 07.02.2013, 14:30]; http://www.listal.com/list/racist-disney [retrieved 07.02.2013, 14:35]; http://anaydena.hubpages.com/hub/Is-Disney-Racist [retrieved 07.02.2013, 14:40]

people, which is inaccurate. [...] It has been done in so many movies over so much time,
people think that's the way we are - and it's just wrong. I can list several other movies
where they have portrayed us as backward, toothless, illiterate people who fart". [see
Scott, 2009, retrieved from http://www.nola.com/
movies/index.ssf/2009/07/animated_character_in_new_disn.html; 07.02.2013; 16:40]

The above analysis and discussion of the movies reviewed showed that to date there are
still a lot of stereotypes to be found in Disney movies. Most of these stereotypes have
not or just slightly changed over the past decades. Although superficially it seems that
progress has been made, at closer inspection a lot of this apparent progress is just a new
dress for old and traded gender roles and ethnic prejudice.

7. Conclusion

My own findings of the stereotypes presented within movies of The Disney Princess franchise are in most parts consistent with what has been said before (Artz 2004, Ayres 2003, Giroux 1995, LaCroix 2004, Manley 2003). Disney continues to present very stereotypical representations of women and men. Girls should be obedient, dutiful and above all beautiful. Men are adventurous, bold and enjoy more freedoms. Although the Disney Princess franchise also includes heroines of other ethnicities, ethnic stereotypes are reproduced and reinforced by the depiction of the antagonists in those movies.

It is also clear that Disney continues to negate today's reality that many children do not live in a 'traditional' family, but rather in one of many possible constellations which can be found in today's society. In combination with the fact that all these love stories postulate a heterosexual normativity, it is apparent that Disney promotes a family ideal, which is outdated and no longer the standard and devaluates living situations, which do not conform to that idea.

While my findings might not present any groundbreaking new results, I do however believe that it highlights new aspects and that the use of the Critical Discourse Analysis as my method opens up new areas of scientific interest.

As I have said in my introduction, a lot of research has already been conducted on Disney films and its stereotypical depictions. Most of the academic literature agrees that the gender and ethnic representations in Disney films are stereotypical. However, throughout my extensive research for this Bachelor's thesis, the question for Disney's motives to keep on repeating the same stories became much more prominent. Unfortunately, I found that very few articles touched the subject as to *why* Disney would have such an agenda.

What many authors seem to forget is that Disney is a corporation. A business, whose image is build around family, happiness, and happily-ever-afters. Wasko (2001) uses a quotation by Walt Disney himself, to reveal "'*one of the keys to Disney's presumed uni-*

versality': "What we've built up in the public mind over the years."' (Jackson, 1993, p. 11 as cited in Wasko, 2001, p. 253)

Disney has been nurturing and controlling its brand for decades now. With time, it has been globally marketed and promoted with the goal to reach people's hearts and minds all over the world. *"The Disney Company has grown and expanded globally by vigilantly controlling their products, characters, and images and by developing their reputation as a company and as a brand that produces positive, wholesome, family and children's entertainment."* (Wasko, 2001, p. 253)

Wasko refers to the Global Disney Audience Project (GDAP), a study that analyzed Disney audiences in eighteen different countries. One of the main findings of the study was that the "essence" of Disney is understood all around the world or as Wasko (2001, p. 253) explains it: *"There seems to be an almost universally accepted awareness of what "Disney" means, as well as a recognition of the basic characteristics of the Classic Disney, [...]."*

Further results of this study show that there are certain core values, which are associated with Disney and Disney products on a global scale. *"More than 93 percent of the respondents agreed that Disney promoted fun and fantasy, while more than 88 percent agreed on happiness, magic, and good over evil. Other terms that ranked very high (in the 80 percent range) were family, imagination, and love and romance."* (Wasko, 2011, p. 254) Whether or not the respondents actually liked Disney was irrelevant.

These numbers show that Disney represents values and ideas, which are received and understood similarly all around the world. Values and ideas, which Disney *"consistently and emphatically insists on in its own self-definition and in its incessant promotion and marketing"*, (Wasko, 2011, p. 254) "[b]*ut in Disney's case, the medium is also the advertisement. Disney products are themselves advertisements for Disney and for its ideological and cultural themes"* (Lee Artz, 2004, p. 140).

Therefore, when it comes to the stereotypical depictions in Disney films, *"Disney does not 'conspire' to build [...] a new world order".* Rather," *it's pro-capitalist ideological premise is patently obvious, redundant and pervasive"* (Lee Artz, 2004, p. 140).

Obviously, producing films, which still include stereotypical depictions in terms of gender and other ethnic groups, seems to be a good business strategy for Disney. Apparently, we as an audience, still wish and long for the black and white world with the guaranteed Happy End. Disney as a company is merely capitalizing on our desires. What we may not forget though, is having been around for over 75 years, Disney has had enough time to *instil* these wishes and desires in us. *"These desires and wishes are not ours – even when we think they are or would like them to be – because we tend to forget what the culture industry does to our children and ourselves."* (Zipes, 1997)

I do not think that we "tend to forget" what the culture industry in general and Disney in particular does to our children or ourselves, I rather believe that we want to ignore it. The study by Feng and Scharrer (2004) presented at the beginning of this paper actually gives all the answers. We suspend criticism and we ignore problematic depictions in order to still be able to feel the *"intense pleasure and fond memories"* when watching the films.

However, can Disney be painted the villain in this story? After all, they do not conceal their goals and motivations. A glance at the Disney Consumer Product Homepage shows us the following description for the Disney Princess franchise: *"For a little girl, the desire to feel special is more powerful than a magic wand. She dreams of a place where clothes are spun of silk and gold, where balls are held in her honor and where princes fall in love at first sight. It is a world Disney has created — full of fantasy and romance — where a girl can feel as special as a princess. Disney Princess – where dreams begin".*

In their essay "The Disadvantage of a Good Reputation: Disney as a Target for Social Problems Claims", Best and Lowney (2009) examine the Disney Corporation as target of criticism. They argue that Disney's good reputation has made it attractive to claims-makers from various social spheres - the academic world, religion or the business world.

However, they come to the result that *"[p]erhaps some parents decide to protect their children from what they become persuaded are pro-homosexual or antiwomen messages in Disney's popular cultural products, but large numbers of parents continue to have confidence in the Disney brand (or at least have not found the various calls for action compelling), and families continue to flock to the Disney parks"*. (Best & Loweney, 2009, p. 445)

But although Disney is a corporation trying to make profits, Disney is also big enough a corporation not only to influence global discourse, but to actually control global discourse. Their movies are marketed to a global and diverse audience. Their main target group is children. Therefore, it is important to see that with such an influence, certain responsibilities come along.

In addition, we can see that Disney does not just simply retell old children's fairy tales and can therefore not be held responsible for the content of the story. In contrast, Disney's motives can be strongly questioned on grounds of why they choose particular stories (with correspondent moral messages) in the first place and also, why they adapt, interpret, and change these stories in certain ways. It also leaves the question on why certain dimensions of diversity are excluded all together.

The issues of gender and ethnicity/race in Disney movies have been the topic of several studies already (Arzt, 2004; Ayres, 2001; Bean, 2001; LaCroix, 2004; Ma, 2001; Towbin et al 2004). However, very few have dealt with the issues of ageism, homosexuality, the portrayal of disabled people or the portrayal of different religions.

In their study, Towbin et al. (20043, p. 40) showed that few themes emerged related to ageism and homophobia. There were no portrayals of same-sex relationship in any of the movies.

Therefore, future studies should focus more on these neglected dimensions. During my research, I found that especially the intersectional interaction between the dimensions age and gender unearths a lot of stereotypical depictions. Also, the complete omittance of same-sex relationship poses an interesting field of further scientific research.

Literature

Allport, G. W. (1954). The nature of prejudice.

Artz, L. (2004). The righteousness of self-centred royals: The world according to Disney animation. Critical Arts: South-North Cultural and Media Studies, 18(1), 116-146.

Axelrod, M. (2003). Beauties and Their Beasts & Other Motherless Tales from the Wonderful World of Walt Disney. In Ayres, B. (Ed.), The Emperor's old Groove: Decolonizing Disney's Magic Kingdom (pp. 29-38). New York, NW: Peter Lang Publishing Inc.

Ayres, B. (2003). The poisonous apple in Snow White: Disney's Kingdom of Gender. In Ayres, B. (Ed.), The Emperor's old Groove: Decolonizing Disney's Magic Kingdom (pp. 39-50). New York, NY: Peter Lang Publishing Inc.

Ayres, B., Hines, S. (2003). (He)gemony Cricket! Why in the World Are We Still Watching Disney?. In Ayres, B. (Ed.), The Emperor's old Groove: Decolonizing Disney's Magic Kingdom (pp. 1-12). New York, NY: Peter Lang Publishing Inc.

Bazzini, D., Curtin, L., Joslin, S., Regan, S., & Martz, D. (2010). Do Animated Disney Characters Portray and Promote the Beauty–Goodness Stereotype?. Journal of Applied Social Psychology, 40(10), 2687–2709. Wiley Periodicals, Inc.

Bean, K. (2003). Stripping Beauty: Disney's "Feminist" Seduction. In Ayres, B. (Ed.), The Emperor's old Groove: Decolonizing Disney's Magic Kingdom (pp. 53-64). New York, NY: Peter Lang Publishing Inc.

Berry, G. L., & Asamen, J. K. (1993). Television and the Developing Child. In a Multimedia World Berry, G.L., & Asamen, J. K. (eds). Children & Television: Images in a Changing Sociocultural world, (pp. 9-37). Cailfornia: SAGE Publications Inc.

Best, J., & Lowey, K. (2009). The Disadvantage of a Good Reputation: Disney as a Target for Social Problems Claims. The Sociological Quarterly 50, 431–449.

Bloomsbury Guide to Human Thought. (1993). Gender. http://www.credoreference.com/entry/bght/genders [retrieved 23.11.2012; 15:24]

Brannon, L. (n.d.) Gender: *Gender. Stereotypes*: Masculinity and Femininity. 159-185. http://www.ablongman.com/partners_in_psych/PDFs/Brannon/Brannon_ch07.pdf; [retrieved 25.11.2012, 18:30]

Bruner, J. S. (1957). On Perceptual Readiness. Psychological Review, 64 (2), 123 -157.

Butler, J. (1990) Gender Trouble. New York, NY: Routledge

Chyng, S. (2001). Mickey Mouse Monopoly [VHS]. Northampton, MA: Media Education Foundation

Connell, R.W. (2002). Gender. Cambridge. Oxford: Polity Press in association with Blackwell Publisher Ltd

Disney Homepage, Segment "Disney Consumer Products", *https://www.disneyconsumerproducts.com/Home/display.jsp?contentId=dcp_home _ourfranchises_disney_princess_us&forPrint=false&language=en&preview=false &imageShow=0&pressRoom=US&translationOf=nul*, [retrieved 25.11.2012, 17:14]

Dotsch, R. (2001). Pictures in our heads: Visual stereotypes affect social categorization. PhD Thesis; PDF hosted at the Radboud Repository of the Radboud University Nijmegen; http://dare.ubn.kun.nl/bitstream/2066/83189/1/83189.pdf [retrieved 24.11.2012, 19:00]

Eagly, A. H., & Steffen, V. J. (1984). Gender Stereotypes Stem From the Distribution of Women and Men Into Social Role. Journal or Personality and Social Psychology, Vol. 46(4), 735-754.

Fairclough, N. (2001). Language and Power (2nd ed). Essex: Pearson Education Limited

Fearon, J. D. (2003). Ethnic structure and cultural diversity around the world. Journal of Economic Growth, 8, 195-222.

Feldman, J. M. (1972). Stimulus characteristics and subject prejudice as determinants of stereotype attribution. Journal of Personality and Social Psychology, 21, 333- 340.

Feng, C. S, & Scharrer, E. (2004). Staying True to Disney: College Students' Resistance to Criticism of The Little Mermaid. The Communication Review, 7(1), 35-55.

Finkelstein, R. (2003). Disney's *Tempest*: Colonizing Desire in *The Little Mermaid.* In Ayres, B. (Ed.), The Emperor's old Groove: Decolonizing Disney's Magic Kingdom (pp. 131-147). New York, NY: Peter Lang Publishing Inc.

Fitch, M., Huston, A. C., & Wright, J.C. (1993). From Television Forms to Genre Schemata: Children's Perceptions of Television Reality. In Berry, G.L., & Asamen, J. K. (eds). Children & Television: Images in a Changing Sociocultural world, (pp. 5-8). Cailfornia: SAGE Publications Inc.

Gardenswarzt, L., & Rowe, A. (2009). The Effective Management of Cultural Diversity. In Moodian, M.A. (ed). Contemporary Leadership and Intercultural Competence, (pp. 35-43). California: SAGE Publications Inc.

Giroux, H.A. (1995). Animating Youth: the Disnification of Children's Culture. Socialist Review 24(3), 23-55. http://www.henryagiroux.com/online_articles/animating_youth.htm [retrieved 12.12.2011, 20:30]

Götz, M., & Schlote, E. (2010). Was ist Diverstiät/Diversity?. Televizion 23/2012(2), 8.

Götz, M., Hofmann, O., Brosius, H.-B., Carter, C., Chan, K., Donal, St. H., … Zhang, H. (2008). Gender in children's television worldwide. Televizion 21/2008(E). 4-9.

Herche, M., & Götz, M. (2008). The global girl's body. Televizion 21/2008(E), 18-19.

Ingwersen, N., & Ingwersen, F. (1990). Splash! Six Views of "The Little Mermaid" – A Folktale Approach. Scandinavian Studies, 62, 412 – 415.

Jackson, K. M. (1993). Walt Disney: A bio-bibliography. Westport, CT: Greenwood

Jäger, S. (2009). Kritische Diskursanalyse: Eine Einführung; Edition DISS, Band 3; 5., gegenüber der 2., überarbeiteten und erweiterten (1999), unveränderte Auflage, Münster 2009, UNRAST-Verlag

LaCroix, C. (2004). Images of Animated Others: The Orientalization of Disney's Cartoon Heroines From The Little Mermaid to The Hunchback of Notre Dame. Popular Communication: The International Journal of Media and Culture, 2(4), 213-229.

Lippmann, W. (1922). Public opinion. Nueva York, Free Press.

Macleod, D. S. (2003). The Politics of Vision: Disney, *Aladdin*, and the Gulf War. In Ayres, B. (Ed.), The Emperor's old Groove: Decolonizing Disney's Magic Kingdom (pp. 179-192). New York, NY: Peter Lang Publishing Inc.

Manley, K. (2003). Disney, the Beast, and Woman as Civilizing Force. In Ayres, B. (Ed.), The Emperor's old Groove: Decolonizing Disney's Magic Kingdom (pp. 79-89). New York, NY: Peter Lang Publishing Inc.

MarketLine (2012), Company Profile: The Walt Disney Company, Reference Code: 8C7AE530-4ECC-4EF5-AC18-370E646FD097, Publication Date: 28 May 2012, www.marketline.com (retrieved on the 25th November 2012 from datamonitor360 http://360.datamonitor.com/Product?pid=8C7AE530-4ECC-4EF5-AC18-370E646FD097, 15:00)

Matyas, V. (2010). TALE AS OLD AS TIME: A Textual Analysis of Race and Gender in Disney Princess Films. Graduate Major Research Papers and Multimedia Projects. Paper 6. http://digitalcommons.mcmaster.ca/cmst_grad_research/6

McGarty, C., Yzerbyt, V. Y., & Spears, R.(2002) Stereotypes as explanations: The formation of meaningful beliefs about social groups. Cambridge, UK: Cambridge University Press

Merriam-Webster online. (n. d.). Diversity. http://www.merriam-webster.com/dictionary/diversity [retrieved 20.11.2012, 15:00]

Minority Rights Group International. MRG. (2009). State of the World's Minorities and Indigenous Peoples. http://www.minorityrights.org/ [retrieved 29.11.2012, 20:15]

Murray, J.P. (1993). The Developing Child in a Multimedia Society. In a Multimedia World Berry, G.L., & Asamen, J. K. (eds). Children & Television: Images in a Changing Sociocultural world, (pp. 5-8). Cailfornia: SAGE Publications Inc.

Popeau, J. (1998). Ethnicity/race. Core Sociological Dichotomies. Jenks, C. (eds) Great Britain: Sage Publication.

Prentice, D. A., & Carranza, E. (2002). What women and men should be, shouldn't be, are allowed to be, and don't have to be: the contents of prescriptive gender stereo-types. Psychology of Women Quarterly, 26 (2002), 269–281. Blackwell Publish-ing. Princeton University

Rosch, E. (1978). Principles of categorization. In E. Rosch & B. B. Lloyd (Eds.), Cog-nition and categorization. Hillsdale, NJ: Erlbaum. Reprinted in: Margolis, E. and Laurence, S. (Eds.) (1999). Concepts: Core readings. Cambridge, MA: MIT Press.

Schlote, E. (2010). Ethnic minorities and migration. Televizion 23/2012(E), 14-15.

Schlote, O. (2010). Kulturelle Vielfalt im Kinderfernsehen. Televizion magazine, 23/2010/2, 9-14.

Signorielli, N. (1993). Television, the Portrayal of Women, and Children's Attitudes. In Berry, G.L., & Asamen, J. K. (eds). Children & Television: Images in a Changing Sociocultural world, (pp. 5-8). Cailfornia: SAGE Publications Inc.

Smedley, J. W., & Bayton, J. A. (1978). Evaluative raceclass stereotypes by race and perceived class of subjects. Journal of Personality and Social Psychology, 36, 530-535.

Soracco, S.L. (1990). Splash! Six Views of "The Little Mermaid" – A Psychoanalytic Approach. Scandinavian Studies, 62, 408 – 412.

Spencer, S. (2006). Race and Ethnicity: Culture, identity and representation. Oxford: Routledge (Taylor & Francis Group)

Tajfel, H. (1969). Cognitive Aspects of Prejudice. Journal of social Issues, 25(4), 79–97.

Tajfel, H. (1981). Human Groups and Social Categories: Studies in Social Psychology. Cambridge, UK: Cambridge University Press.

Triandis, H. C. (1977). Interpersonal behavior. Monterey, CA: Brooks/Cole.

Van Berghe, P. L. (1967). Race and Racism: A Comparative Perspective. New York, NW: John Wiley & Sons

Van Dijk, T.A. (2001). Critical Discourse Analysis. In D. Tannen, D. Schiffrin, & H. Hamilton (Eds.), Handbook of Discourse Analysis. (pp. 352-371). Oxford: Black-well

Washington, D. (2008). The concept of Diverstity. http://dwashingtonllc.com/images/pdf/publications/the_concept_of_diversity.pdf [retreived 22.11.2012, 17:00]

Wasko, J. (2001). Challenging Disney Myths. Journal of Communication Inquiry, 25(3), 237-257.

Wellner, A. (2000), unknown

Yzaguirre, C. (2006). A whole new world? The evolution of Disney animated heroines from Snow White to Mulan. http://scholarship.shu.edu/cgi/viewcontent.cgi?article=1506&context=dissertations [retrieved 10.12.2012, 21:00]

Zipes, J. (1997). Happily Ever After: Fairy Tales, Children and the Culture Industry. NY: Routledge

Popular Sources

Wikipedia www.wikipedia.org

The Disney Wiki http://disney.wikia.com/wiki/The_DisneyWiki

Disney Consumer Products www.disneyconsumerproducts.com

Snow White and The Seven Dwarfs (movie)

Cinderella (movie)

Sleeping Beauty (movie)

The Little Mermaid (movie)

Beauty and the Beast (movie)

Aladdin (movie)

Pocahontas (movie)

Mulan (movie)

The Princess and The Frog (movie)

Tangled (movie)

Pictures

http://www.univie.ac.at/diversity/146.html

https://www.disneyconsumerproducts.com/Home/display.jsp?contentId=dcp_home_our

fran-

chises_disney_princess_us&forPrint=false&language=en&preview=false&imageShow

=0&pressRoom=US&translationOf=nul&region=0&first=0&last=0

http://images.wikia.com/disney/images/2/25/New-disney-princess-lineup-
rapunzeldisney-princess-18212648-1280-800.jpg

http://disney.wikia.com/wiki/File:S-16_SnowWhite2.png

http://disney.wikia.com/wiki/File:Dibujo203.1.jpg

http://disney.wikia.com/ wiki/File:12357.gif

http://disney.wikia.com/wiki/File:Gaston.jpg

http://i19.photobucket.com/albums/b191/AladdinsGenie/For%20Friends/aladdin005295

.png

http://images4.wikia.nocookie.net/__cb20120413171941/villains/images/5/50/Shanyu_r

ef_%281%2911.jpg

http://images2.fanpop.com/image/photos/10900000/tiana-and-naveen-after-wedding-
the-princess-and-the-frog-10977173-1280-800.jpg

http://disney-clipart.com/Aladdin/jasmine/Princess-Jasmine3.php

http://disney.wikia.com/wiki/Pocahontas_%28character%29

http://disney.wikia.com/wiki/Rapunzel

http://disney.wikia.com/wiki/File:Mulanaspingart.png

http://disney.wikia.com/wiki/Ray?file=Princess-And-The-Frog-Ray.jpg

stills from the movies

Televizion magazine (23/2010/E)

Televizion magazine (21/2008/E)

Televizion magazine (23/2010/2)

CPSIA information can be obtained
at www.ICGtesting.com
Printed in the USA
BVHW031132250820
587259BV00001B/168